PROLOGUE	4
PART ONE	10
PART TWO	62
PART THREE	111
PART FOUR	163

BRONZE AGE MINDSET
AN EXHORTATION

BY
BRONZE AGE PERVERT

This book dedicated to the memory of Dean Dejana, a spiritual brother, a Sardinian giant of high vision, man of superhuman physical strength. You were too strong for this world, friend. Be reborn in a better time—we meet again, we fight together!

VICTORY TO THE GODS!

PROLOGUE

This is not book of philosophy. It is exhortation. I hardly have anything to say to most who aren't like me, still less do I care about convincing. This is account of my reveries. I tried to put, as brief and simple as I could, the thought that motivates me and the problem faced by life in ascent and decline.

I was convinced to write this book by certain frogs who told me, "Is it not a shame that hucksters are multiplying lies, and jizzing their filthy doctrines into receptive minds everywhere? Perversions—*lame* ones—are born by the thousands and haunt, like myriad cripplette midgets in halls of mirrors, they haunt the world, books, the internet. Minds are lost. If you wait any longer everything will be pounded to garbage, there will be nothing left—it will all turn, the whole world will turn to a Bulgarian rest stop lavatory. But have you *seen* the movie *Midnight Express*...and...and how did it make you *feel?*"

I was roused from my slumber by my frog friends and I declare to you, with great boldness, that I am here to save you from a great ugliness.

If you look around eyes of some people you see a kind of demented energy. It's pure anger or lust for power with nothing more. I hate to dirty these pages with mention of names of nobodies in our time. But if you see photo of Hillary Clintong or Adam Schiff with his eyes bugged out on stims and antidepressants or who knows what, you know what I mean. There is a crease around the eye that tells it, it looks like cyborg gone off-script, these people have an inhuman gaze and are vehicles for something else. You see this also in the chiefs of the EU bureaucracy with tiny moleman eyes behind small glasses, and the tiny lenses that reflect light. You see it in the dead robot eyes of the new hue-man automatons running government departments, the DMV, the brutal zombies running the security in airports or hospital "health care" rooms under vicious yellow fluorescent lights.

I wanted to expose the grim shadow of a movement that is hidden behind events of our time and from before. This is a great power that acts like a ghost. It hides in its own darkness and it has been absorbed by the lands and the peoples so that you can't really see it anymore. There is just an eldritch quality embedded in things and on some faces. The same was said of Hades. Some said he would feel a great shame when some other god drew back the veil on the underworld so all the vile things that are there could be seen. Is this Hades of our time capable of shame? I heard also of such things being under the sea, the disgusting and frightful things revealed when the sea recedes before a great storm. I will draw back the curtain on this Iron Prison and show you where it is you *really* live...

The secret things show in dreams. Heraclitus say, "All the things you see awake are death, all the things you see asleep are sleep." He was trying to be coy! In his day many gods, clove-footed satyr, and other things showed themselves to men in dreams.

Spiritually your insides are all wet, and there's a huge hole through where monstrous powers are fucking your brain, letting loose all your life and power of focus. You don't see yourself as you really are, but maybe some nightmare can show it to you. I am here to show you the way out.

There was Empedocles, a philosopher, man of high vision. He jumped into volcano Aetna in Sicily because he knew he would be reborn as a god. Now imagine yourself in front of rim of Aetna. It's dry and sandy. You feel the heat but is not like you thought it might be. Is not Romantic. Is just hot, dry, you can't breathe, and the smell of infernal sulfur and wet earth and even worse things triggers an old memory or instinct in you to run. You're brought to face with a vehemence and brutality of rock and you start to feel dizzy staring in. Molten rock in your nostrils and it's not just that it scares you. If it were great fear, that could be a spur to action. But it fills your nostrils with banality and dullness of plain molten dust, you see gray and black. It reminds you of torrid summer afternoon by abandoned gas station, you are stranded on dirt road, choked by heat and so much dust. You see flames in the hole but it lacks the romance of fire as you imagined it. Is this it? It seems like nothing to you, because to your eye it's nothing. So you pull away from it. You're not reborn as a god, you remain a mule. Your lying mind now comes up with many thoughts about why it's right to pull back. Why, of course! There's a nice meal to have, a glass of wine. Maybe there's a girl waiting. Her pussy is warm and inviting. Empedocles was deluded.

No, don't jump in Aetna or Mauna Loa or Puyehue or Eyjafjallajökull, Titans of the world, even if you get yourself to do it, it won't work now. These portals are closed for ages. But! Other doors are closed to you too. What Mount Aetna was to Empedocles—is there something like that to you? Is there something like that at all anymore?

Life has a thing inside it that reaches beyond itself. This is intergalactic worm, I can't say here, you must wait. But if you don't reach beyond yourself you are dead! Most of mankind is the walking dead.

I tell you other story. In Stone Age man appears, very strong shoulders, with club in hand. He is believed by the people to be a son of some god...of a mortal woman who cucked her husband with a god. As child he already displays superhuman strength. When he grows he goes into the deepest wild to fight great cave lion. He emerges from cave with skin of lion on his back. Lion had been eating and working terror in the people, but now he wears this terror on his shoulders. He carries lion mane on head, lion pelt on back and a great club in the hand. This man comes to be worshiped by the people: his progeny become lines of kings, of Sparta and many other places. What was his act of foundation? He slaughtered monsters, he made the seaways known to man and tamed the rock-face. But don't forget the lion-skin on his shoulders. This was lion of Nemea. Do you understand what Nemesis is? There is in nature a great purgative function. You know about monkeys who switch sex in certain times. In lake of some reptiles, when they overpopulate it and there is a surplus of refuse, there is trigger in nature: a monster is born to them. A lizard many times the size of a normal one is born, who deals out destruction and culls the lake. The Greeks believed in this great power and worshiped its justice. In Bible it appears as allegory of the Flood, which in fact refers to the irrepressible spirit of the Sea Peoples, and the divine justice they brought to cities whose life had grown pointless, and a great ugliness on the world. You bring lion cub into the house, but Aeschylus say, it will become a priest of doom when it reaches age: in nature there is irrepressible force. Its violence against the surfeit of populations is divine justice. Its destruction of the feeble designs of reason, the pointless words of man—this is beautiful. This what the power of Nemesis means: few are chosen to wield it, fewer realize they are chosen or know what to do with it. When Hercules puts on the power of Nemesis on his shoulders he becomes hero who makes the world tame and safe for cities of real men. But that was in his time, and ours is an age of surfeit. It is different function. The star of Nemesis is sure to return, and it must already be burning inside some of you.

In the Bronze Age men had life and *force,* and I already see, far on the horizon of our world, but the glimmer is surely there—may it not be a mirage!—I see this spirit returning surely in our time. Piratical bands and brotherhoods will take to the seas, and not just to the seas. The enemies of Western man and the enemies of beauty are to learn just what was meant by a *piratical race,* a nest of pirates like the Chinese thought of the Dutch on first meeting them. I want to prepare you to receive this old spirit—old spirits are moving, from behind the reeds... the silhouette shimmers against a river in late summer, and I see already men who know how to honor such uncanny old friends.

May they inhabit us again and give us strength to purify this world of refuse

Part One: The Flame of Life

1

What if you've been misled about what is life? They do this by showing you two red marionette and shake them in front, then you stay mesmerized and clap like trained seal. Is like in politics before last year. You had in years before Trump, the fat bald gluttons of the Right put in a fighting ring against the Janet Renos, the womyn with pickup trucks, the thin-lipped transnumales of the Left. You had good people mesmerized even by this show: and it's funny to see a fat bald man try to tear out the eyes of woman of strong forearm with mullet, both frothing at mouth. Both saying nothing, but grunts of pigs and pre-made platitude, formula. But meanwhile the nation suffered and the future of youth was given away. When they trick you about what is life, this even worse because you don't see problem right away... but then comes out sixty years later and your grandchildren don't exist, or they are 56% humanoid shifting about between shadows, or they are of noble power but have to hide under half-finished buildings because are hunted. But you must understand both left and right have been fooled about what is life.

2

Group of horses in broad plain, and the lead stallion is captured by a wild spirit, starts to gallop this way and that, and the whole herd follows in a great rush of power and freedom—Nietzsche talks about this. I've seen many things like this myself: was at big waterfall, gathering place of many birds and other animal. Through all the cycles of history this place remains and birds who witnessed the coming and going of human civilizations remember it through the aeons and always return there. I saw many group of small birds, when the weather slightly changed, this waterfall so big that a small wind would make spray of water everywhere. Sun came from behind clouds and spread many small rainbows, birds would become excited, come out from crevasses in rock face and would glory in the sprays of water and the rainbows, they swoon doing acrobatics this way and that. Like when Homer says that on some Asian meadow tribes of geese, and crane and long-necked swans glory in the power of their wings above it, then land between the rivers, in Skamandrian plain, with a great clang. Is not enough just to say, what is purpose of this to survival or reproduction? Surely some pedant can make a story. But when you see this behavior, is not so alien. Maybe, in happiest moments you were free to act and feel the same: what anything to do with survival or reproduction! That kind of heavy necessity is the spirit of gravity, and this is opposite. That petty and cramped view of life...but in truth, life as it is, when free, life in abundance knows luxury, surfeit and waste...survival and reproduction are side effects of something else...

3

The most noble animals refuse to breed in captivity. Many animal, not just man, choose death when trapped. But I thought all life strove for mere survival and reproduction; but this not enough? But if not enough then must understand animal in some other way. Very much when thinkers talk about "evolutionary psychology" they abstract from way of yeast to way of animals and man, but this is backward.

4
There's a sociology of the world of scientists like of everything else. This is a cause of much confusion about biology and ideas of evolution. You think you've been given objective truth, but the minds of biologists are in general very limited. The truth is the biggest minds always went for physics among the sciences, then maybe chemistry. Until recently but even now biology gives little opportunity for the kind of thinking that penetrates mystery of nature, the kind of insight into physical relations that attracts the best scientific minds. They've been on the whole a half-and-half group in history. Schopenhauer refers with contempt to the people who have their "catalogues of monkeys" and think they understand nature. Darwin himself, Nietzsche called him a petty mind, the kind of calculator who likes to collect many small facts and synthesize some clumsy theory. The theory is clumsy and full of holes. This is the biggest reason Creationists, who are also wrong, have been able to challenge it, where they were never able to challenge theoretical physics. There is much dishonesty and stupidity among scientists and biologists when they talk about evolution and life.

5
The problem now is you think I want to attaq idea of evolution or to change it because it's racist or uncomfortable, just like the left and others attaq or suppress it. This is not true! Listen: you don't *need* Darwin to believe in heredity and even evolution. People knew about heredity and the different lineages of man long before Darwin. In the political sense the

promotion of Darwin teaching and its application to mankind is a great good. The left and its many robots—I will talk of their origin later—want nothing more than to hide truth about human nature. And Darwin, evolutionary science in all its forms, is a great weapon of truth against them. In all this I agree, but remember the marionettes I mentioned. Don't be distracted by the puppet play. It is important not to be misled by a fierce debate with a stupid opponent into just accepting the only other alternative that is presented to you. Although the left, or what I have termed the Bug-man, hates and fears evolutionary ideas applied to humans, Darwinism itself is the product of bug-thought. In the end it won't show you way out of the prison of the ages. The hereditary nature of the qualities, and the suitability of an organism to its environment and vice-versa, all of this is true observation. And that true observation about heredity is in the end enough: you don't *need* more than that to utterly crush all the designs and vanities of the Bug-man. The Bugman fears heredity and nature, not Darwin.

6

You must understand that the evolutionary psychologist, the evo-biologist, the Darwinist in general—most such people are very good, and even great minds, who are just misled by the fight—plays a game of bait-and-switch. Many times he's not aware he does this himself. He believes in Darwinism as a teleological faith, that reproduction and survival are the *ends* of life, the purpose toward which all life strives and that this explains how life or an organism behaves; and also how it is adapted to its environment. But when you confront him on this, he will deny all notion of teleology. He will say he doesn't believe in any of this, but only in a material mechanism of natural selection. Through this mechanism those organisms that are not in keeping with demands of environment at some time are slowly pared out. By a process analogous to our breeding of animals like dog and horse, nature itself breeds organisms and life this way and that, by accident. There is no end or purpose, he will say, you are crazy! But then when he's not paying attention he will talk a different way. They all do this. He will start to say that this or that animal is behaving this or that way because it is trying to secure either reproduction or survival. He will explain physical features in this way too, and when he really forgets himself he will make a moral principle out of it. The most honest ones, when they trust you, will talk about replicating themselves as an aspiration and a goal. This is human, all-too-human but also very natural, because it's very hard to talk about biology or life without teleology or some consideration of ends or purpose. Clearly physics and chemistry seem to be driven by no purpose or goal. But animals seem very much driven by motive or purpose, and is hard to explain a biological feature without reference to its end or purpose. So the Darwinist forgets, or tries to change the topic all the time: he knows what is really interesting is the question of what drives life, what explains animal behavior and what explains the correspondence between organism and environment. This is the question. The mechanism of heredity or the means by which a species is shaped, natural or unnatural selection, which is really Darwin's only insight, is the least interesting part of all. Actually it is a tautology: yes, only those animals who have managed to reproduce actually pass on their traits. Something every sheep breeder in history has known. But that this alone explains animal adaptation or behavior is nonsense.

7

There is Alpine mouse that collects food for winter. Somehow it knows exactly the proportion of poison herbs to include in winter stores, to preserve them. Too much, and the food it gathered becomes poison, too little and it spoils. There is example Schopenhauer gives: two insects, and one will kill the other on sight. Yet this other presents no immediate danger to the first, but will only eat its eggs in the future. How does that first insect know this? It is not taught, nor does it see. It has very primitive nervous system. It knows this somehow "in the blood." This is a very specific and complicated behavior. There are many such cases in nature! Creationists have focused too much on complicated physical features, but even for something like the eye or the bacterial flagellum it is possible to construct stories of how they evolved gradually. I don't believe those stories, they sound improbable and made-up, but they're more believable than the stories you have to make up in the case of behaviors. And many more! So many animals and simple insects have such complicated behaviors they are born with already. At some point the incremental explanation becomes so convoluted it is hard to believe. Please remember that Aristotelian-Ptolemaic system for calculating motion of planets and so on worked quite well for long time. It was abandoned because ever more convoluted explanations had to be invented to support the fundamental and wrong assumption of geocentric model. Evolutionary theory today is slowly in same position, and nowhere more than where they may try to explain inborn behaviors of this kind. It is obvious that such behaviors—if you want to call them "adaptations"—came about as we see them now, complete and without significant incremental change. How did such "miracle" occur? This is not Creationist book—I do not believe in that. Nor do I believe in the "miracle" that modern science has invented, hiding under the word "random mutation" and the hand-waving of "incremental change." There is not enough *time,* nor enough number of specimens, nor the kinds of "mutations" observed to support either natural selection or Lamarckianism as explanations for evolution. Many of the mathematical models for how a trait will spread in a population have failed—they don't tell you this. No, I don't talk about miracles, whatever words you put them under. And the "design" is there, but it is by no means benevolent or intelligent, nor comprehensible. You see in the spider's web a creature of rudimentary nervous system and little intelligence "design" something beautiful and complex, and this is key to understanding also all of nature. There is an inherent "intelligence" inside things, uncanny, silent and demonic. Its workings and aims are obscure to us. Our own intelligence is only a crude deviation of it, an approximation. There is an "intelligence" in all things, and inborn in our bodies before anything to do with the brain or the nervous system. And all "adaptations," no matter how much natural or unnatural selection may have gone to spreading them within a population, occur not by random but by a spontaneous correspondence of some kind between the organism and the environment. Some day we may discover the material cause or manifestation of this correspondence, or the chain by which it travels from the rock-face and the elements of brute matter up the forms of life—there is some as-yet undiscovered "signaling" system. But the adaptation by no means takes place at random, nor even primarily by natural selection, which is just one of the means by which it spreads in a population.

8

A truly objective or scientific approach to life would be to start without assumptions. Make no big stories. Take animal and study. Study what it does *in nature,* not lab, when left alone from human. Study different specimens, the mood, the behavior at different time of year, in different places, at different levels of fortune and well-being. Make no assumption about what it wants *ultimately,* study how it behave today, tomorrow, *in the moment,* which is only thing that exists for animal. Look inside its brain! Study its hormones and its internal states with great care, and, with clinical objective eye, correlate these internal states to what it does, or what it's driving at—and driving at *that day* or in that moment, not what you think about "reproduction or survival." This is true path to understand animal, adaptation, behavior and *life.* There is some of this done, but much too little, and not well. In the end, are you so different from goat, dog or even *ant* that you look at such beings and really remain puzzled? For sure the real research I just named must be done, if only to convince the boneheads. But the behavior of an animal would be a complete mystery to you if you weren't very similar yourself; but we understand right away a bear angry at bees, or playing under white-silver birch in thick of forest, or lizard frightened and winding between rocks, why it does what it does. It is no mystery to us, who are also like them. We love dogs because they express so honestly and without dissimulation what we also are and want. They and other pets calm us because promote a kind of carelessness normal to animal life, unencumbered by thoughts of the past or worries about the future, none of which actually exist. Women are, in their natural state, close to this condition as well, or closer on the whole, which is where they get much of their charm and power from (the modern education, that teaches women to be hyper-aware, anxious for the future, abstract neurotics, etc., actually takes away their power to a great degree, while tricking them into thinking they are being tough or sassy; but a hyper-conscious woman is made powerless and charmless). But study must be made of inner state of animal, now in this condition, now that. What anyway would objective study of an organism say? What does life want?

9

Darwin and his style of thinking would never have made so much impression or ever had such power if it were simply false. Actually Darwinism is true, but only under certain conditions. It's not even a "half-truth," it's actually the full truth about a *kind* of life, but the mistake is to think it describes all life. Darwin is meaningless without Malthus, but this is why Nietzsche is right about both of them when he says they describe only life in England, or more precisely the England of that time. The beginning of the industrial age, and England as the first nation that solved the problem of infant mortality: these are the relevant facts. England was able to colonize so much of the New World because it was the first country to solve this problem. Many criticize in some way the Spanish or Portuguese model of colonization but you must know the Portuguese had a population of one million when they began the age of discovery with Henry the Navigator. And of that population, many fewer were young men who could embark on voyages of great danger; some say up to a fourth or more died on these voyages alone. They had no manpower to settle faraway lands but continued the old pattern of "elite dominance," where brotherhoods of conquering men often took local wives and such. By contrast the English could now transplant entire populations, being surfeit of huemans. But it was still not enough. The cities became crowded, the filth unbearable as the lowest classes swarmed the monstrous new machines of industry. The living conditions of workers well into the 20th Century were purely hellish: Marx and his followers, at least, were right about *that,* and that's why they could prey on this condition. It was a condition of misery and destitution similar to or worse than we see in the shantytowns of the Turd World. Solution to infant mortality problem meant these lower classes put all excess income into supporting more mouths to feed, not improving the quality of life of the children they had: just an exponential increase in human biomass! And this is the world of Malthus and of Darwin, life under filth, life under *distress.* Darwinism describes life under extreme stress. From this very partial view he thinks he has discovered the truth about life in general, but animal under conditions of extreme stress, crowded condition, observed and watched, filthy, beaten and imprisoned, its life severely regimented away from what it would like to do if left to its devices, will not give you secret to what life is. It will be very misleading example, and this is basis of Darwinism and of all thought that comes from it. It is the philosophy of life of the tenement and the slum, of the open air work-camp.

10

No kind of distress is worse than the feeling you are trapped. My worst nightmares are about opening a door only to find myself in the same aluminum cell, over and over. The exhaustion that sets in after a long night of chess, when you sleep and your mind dreams repeat nonsense moves, I know of few worse forms of torment. And this is self-imposed, through exhaustion, but even worse is when an outside force or being restrains you, yet you are in full control of your spirits and power, at least to begin with. That condition is intolerable for the most noble animals, who choose death if necessary, or at least any way to escape no matter how painful. Many Caribs, trapped into slavery, died because they couldn't endure this, some bit through their arms to escape their chains and endured any pain to escape captivity. Germanic mothers would kill infants when Roman legions closed in: Tacitus describe life of Germanic warrior, who lived his whole life dedicated to war and fame, never became a domestic! At Masada and at other times the Jews killed their own children to escape subjection, when they were still a noble people. Xenophon describes in *Anabasis* how mother with infant would jump off a cliff in the highlands of Urartu, to escape the advance of the Greek army: we see same videos in Japan in Okinawa, mother jump off cliff. Buddhist monks Vietnam self-immolated and brought great shame on the West. For this reason Nietzsche say, noble peoples do not endure slavery, they're either free or they die out. There is no "adaptation" to slavery for some types of life. What is that people, who has chosen survival at any price? The price they paid was monstrous and such a people becomes monstrous and distorted if it accepts this. The distinction between master races and the rest is simple and true, Hegel said it, copying Heraclitus: those peoples who choose death rather than slavery or submission in a confrontation, that is a people of masters. There are many such in the world, not only among the Aryans, but also the Comanche, many of the Polynesians, the Japanese and many others. But animal of this kind refuses entrapment and subjection. It is very sad to witness those times when such animal can neither escape nor kill itself. I saw once a jaguar in zoo, behind a glass, so that all the bugs in hueman form could gawk at it and humiliate it. This animal felt a noble and persistent sadness, being observed everywhere by the obsequious monkeys, not even monkeys, that were taunting it with stares. He could tell—I saw this! He could tell he was living in a simulated environment and that he had no power to move or live. His sadness crushed me and I will always remember this animal. I never want to see life in this condition!

11

Just a few weeks ago I was outside night club in city that is still untouched by first-world regimented hygiene: well-lighted, clean streets made safe for women come at a high price for the mood of a city. In this place the government and bureaucracy couldn't extend its rules and cleanup efforts even if it wanted. There are then many nooks and hidden corners that are under no one's control. In this no-man's land there is mafia, so many perverts, there is some crime, but it's kept at mostly very low or nonviolent level because place is full of off-duty cops on the make and no doubt spooks foreign and domestic, and who knows what else. I find life without such refuge to be almost intolerable, so here I felt free but I think was after day in a haze and the glycine was kicking in. I must have taken 600 mg theanine as well, and after much coffee I was spacing out... under vicious neon yellow lights I stood looking at the bouncer almost in a trance. I wondered what it was like to be him. He was alert, knew what posture to take for his job and what look in the eye to emulate... or put on an act of being vigilant, and was imposing in broad frame under leather jacket with military-type epaulettes, but there was a kindness or softness in his eyes. Maybe would have taken some power of perception to see this, and I doubt he was challenged often by the customer riffraff because of it, but I could see it, how at times he sunk into a sadness and boredom looking in the distance. I too looked down the long broad street, mostly empty except for some small groups of drunks, hookers, some revelers, in the distance there was great fountain in plaza lighted up on all sides. I don't know why, maybe the calmness of the blessed aminos hit me but my gaze veered off to one of the apartment buildings on the side of the road. There was just one light turned on in the middle of building and my mind wandered to who lived there and what they were like, and then to how it would be if I was the boy or girl who lived there. Many times I've wished, not so much that I was someone else, nor that I was immortal, but that I could live many different lives simultaneously and not be limited to being only one thing. At such moments of mood where you're both calm and at least *feel* free every detail of life becomes interesting, all takes the character of images from a peaceful dream that present themselves in turn and don't move you one way or another, because you see through them. I wonder then at least as a zoological experiment what it would be like to be a Vietnamese girl, a nail shop owner, or even an obese Angolan middle-aged woman running a pedicure operation with pink walls...yes, no form of hueman life is beneath me at such moments. I've even had dreams that I was a door or a vase, free to observe—I imagine only the seeing, the satisfaction of curiosity, and not the thousands of cares that must affect these people who I want to inhabit. But most of all then, when to this love of curiosity is added some sudden burst of energy, I start to wonder about men like myself of around my age, and what it would be like to be them, what they think moment to moment, what pulls them this way and that. I feel then a great longing for them and also for myself, and think of the friendships that I could have had with them and the great tasks that could await. I feel beset by this as an almost erotic irritation that is diffuse, and a great sadness and irritation that I will never know who lived in that building at that window, never see what they saw looking out. These ways...this is all my version of "love for mankind." Of the other abstract kind, it means nothing and those who invoke it are bullshitters.

12

Very young rams, very young stag even when fawn, well before horns appear, play-fight with heads butting. This is in anticipation of horns that will grow. Yet no one teaches them this, but they know it in the blood. What came "first" for this animal, the development of horns or the "knowledge" and *will* to fight in this manner? In phenomenon like this is kept the secret and truth about evolution and life.

13

Struggle for space—A healthy animal not under distress, not maimed, not trapped by man, seeks first when young: space. Animal seeks space in physical sense, territory. But this meaning isn't crudely physical, I give this as vivid image which is true for many animals that seek ownership of concrete territory. But more generally you must take it to mean something else, space to develop inborn powers. Monkey that lives in trees seeks skills to master canopy, beaver seeks ownership of river and banks and reeds in its grasp, many big cat of course seek mastership of actual territory and claims to prey and mates in this territory. Big feline, hunting dogs seek full use of claws, fangs, development of smell and other senses, to extend their reach over space. They seek these things because they want to master *matter.* All of this is higher organism organizing itself to master matter in surrounding space. Successful mastery of this matter leads to development of inborn powers and flourishing of organism, which allows it to master more matter, to marshal the lower to feed the higher. It is mobilization of matter to develop the inborn character or idea or fate—this true not only for food literally. In social animals an analogous process takes place within social relations or social "space": there are some important changes that happen here, but principle is same. Important to understand that there is a circular process: organism seeks mastery of space, environment, to master matter in ways particular to its own abilities, and as a result of this mastery of matter there is development of its body, its senses, and all of its faculties, and the unfolding of its inborn destined form or nature, in time, its particular form flowering in the spring of its season. All of this requires precisely freedom from struggle for survival, or time away from this, a reprieve from this pressure. As for reproduction, animal in natural state will not even seek at this point, will not even think it. Very far from its aims: it seeks to become strong, skillful, to master problems and feel the expansion of its powers, and not just feel them, but perceive it to be truly so, perceive intuitively its mastery over its space. Only after full development of its powers and its mastery over space specific to its needs does the need or desire for reproduction come. Reproduction is side effect of animal desire for discharge of strength, *after* mastery over space is achieved. For this reason many lower animal breed very fast and in great hurry, but the higher and more organized the form of life, the more complex its needs for development are, the longer is delayed the time of reproduction and the more vulnerable it is to the stresses of competition for survival. Animals that have "evolved" under intense competition are in some sense "stunted," less beautiful, less intelligent, less magnificent. There are many "factions" in nature and many paths that pull in opposite directions. You must learn to see the secret language of nature and what it drives at: there is one path that drives for the production of a supreme specimen. It is the path that governs higher life; survival and reproduction are *only side effects of this path.* Life is at most basic, struggle for ownership of *space.*

14

Some things make my blood boil far more than a direct physical challenge might. I once left the gym and some Chad came up to me and started to feel me up. Then I discovered he was feeling up my pockets, was trying to see if someone stole his missing stuff. I found this very amusing. Maybe was post-workout and I was very calm, but was not offended by this, partly his manner was not obtrusive despite what he was doing. It was possibly a form of muscle worship. But rarely do I feel angrier as a violation of my privacy than if I eat in restaurant alone and someone comes to sit right next to me when the whole place is empty. Vilest of all is when a group of something, I think were subcons or Han, came and sat just by me in entirely empty restaurant and started to eat with mouths open. That sound too, fewer things grate on the nerves and present themselves as imposition on your space than the sound of so-called hue-man eating. Other animals making sound eating don't bother me, but I find charming. Different types even within same grouping of animals—I refuse the word *species*—have very different needs of life. My blood starts to boil, against my kindness and judgment, even when I stay with gril and she insists on setting air conditioner off or closing window because "too cold." I like open spaces and slightly cool, and there can be no living together with creatures who like a huddled and over-warm existence. I believe also the white race, or rather some groupings within it—there are far more races than people want to admit—is in general hostile to the way of life of the tribes that like a close-packed existence. These are biological requirements of this or that way of life, and no laws, no common beliefs, can bring such different types together. A hybrid of such types would probably be born and remain physiologically confused or sick.

15

Whoremoans: Energy and higher life the same—If we had very advanced sensors where we could observe the inside of animals from far and in great detail, without interfering, without them feeling irritated or oppressed by our impositions, we could learn much about what life means. From observing many different ones in different places we could see what conditions an animal seeks in life in general. Such sensors would need to be much more advanced than equipment we have now, and to show what parts of the brain are activated, to see the relationship of this to blood pressure and heart rate, the actions of the immune system, the level of various inflammatory and anti-inflammatory markers, and most of all the balance and action of the various hormones on the body's systems, on the brain, and how these correlate to what the animal is doing at any one time. Any information we have right now on this subject is at most rudimentary. The medical literature is confused, is presented with great confidence, but is corrupted by money, career, and other interests of all kinds. The scientific literature is less known, and itself remains contradictory. We know at most a few relations of what, say, elevated thyroid or cortisol means at such and such time of day, and its multiple effects on various body tissues and systems. We have no real overall understanding of how such things interact, nor what they mean for the body's overall processes, still less in the life of an organism as a whole, and the few who have attempted to achieve such understanding, like Ray Peat, are treated as cranks. But it's not possible to understand what life means, nor what an organism drives at, nor what any specific behavior or physical adaptation means until this is taken up. If biologists had been honest people they would have tried to proceed in this way, without assumptions, just amassing observations about different organisms in different situations. But they did this only very little, and it's always distorted by their various agendas and prejudices. The data we have itself is therefore at this point much too sparse and it will take decades to get what is needed even if researchers begin now. It will be a genius of the ages who will really be able to understand and explain the complete view of how hormones act in an organism. There is no irony here: I don't do irony! Learn that I don't understand the gay idea of "irony." Hormones hold the key to the meaning of life in the most fundamental way, and if this sounds "reductionist" to you, if you think I demystify things too much, it's because you think you know what you don't, or you think scientists know, when they actually don't. These substances, seen with fresh eyes, are pure Big Magic. They govern all cycles of an organism's growth and its decay. They can turn small calf or baby gorilla into giant elephant or half-ton silverback on diet of greens, they can turn skinny man into Herculean half-god or make strong man take on the aspect of woman, and change tendencies and feelings, mirroring the magical transformation of some animals that switch sexes by signals we don't yet understand. This doesn't even begin to cover the different meanings of thyroid, progesterone, the various neurotransmitters, and many others that act one way on the nervous system, another way on the gut, another way on the immune system, that govern cell division and the preservation of function in ways that are for the moment a mystery to doctors and to science. Only a complete understanding of these hidden substances will reveal the fullness of life in its glory! The study of life as a "black box" has led to misunderstandings because the observers are dishonest and stupid and will report an action, but not what comes before or after, nor its place in the life of an animal, nor do they try to intuit from within themselves: the study of hormones, among many other internal processes of an organism, will prevent them from lying in this way. For example, an animal may act one way under stress and pressure, but then appear to do the same action out of a spirit of openness and self-increase, and the same action or behavior may actually have completely different meanings biologically: this will be shown by actions of hormones, neurotransmitters, cytokines in the body. And I will tell you what they likely to discover! So far only Ray Peat, a man blessed by a grand and alien understanding, has tried to decipher the secret language of these blessed substances. Learn that there are at least two kinds of life. Usually you think of life versus inanimate matter—how strange that the most primitive languages, the agglutinative grunts of Neanderthals like Basque, distinguish not between gender of noun, but between animate and inanimate! I wonder then what they would call *yeast*. Learn that there are two kinds of life, and yeast is different from higher life. Higher life means many fancy and mysterious things too of course but at its most basic it has to do with differentiation and structure. Yeast is an "amorphous blob" that expands, whereas a higher organism has different parts with different functions, different organs, different systems within itself. The sexes are different because it reproduces sexually, and some have taken this to be the main distinction, asexual versus sexual reproduction. But it's obvious that "differentiation" in higher organisms goes much beyond this. And to preserve the function of the different organs and different systems within itself, an organism *sacrifices* the ability to expand and replicate indiscriminately, like yeast does for example. You can think of it as "sacrifice" of this ability, or just say that these two modes or tendencies, expansion and replication of cells on one hand, and preservation of higher or differentiated function on the other, are at odds with each other. They are governed by different hormones and neurotransmitters, where estrogen and serotonin are "stress" substances that govern cell division, but thyroid and progesterone are those that govern the preservation of function. It is not correct to call estrogen then a "sex hormone," but a stress hormone, and its greater proportion in body of female is because female is under greater stress due to demands of inner cell division and menstruation. The picture is far from complete of course, but this leads to many good observations. Considering this from the other side, the side of pathology, the indiscriminate cell division, the return of "primitive life" within the human body is called cancer, which looks and acts very much like a fungus does. Conversely, from the side of health, the structure of the body is preserved to the extent that cells successfully command energy, and so, to speak artistically but to be right, on one side the hormones that promote cell energy are precisely those that promote the preservation of function, namely thyroid and the like, whereas the hormones that promote "lassitude" and that take away energy are precisely those that promote cell division,

30

inflammation, the production of free radicals, the breakdown in order and function. At a deep level this must be connected to the fundamental truth of nature, that structure and energy must be the same, that energy is not as "diffuse" as we imagine it, but has an inner "intelligence"—this word is very bad in this case, because it is rather the imperfect intellect of our brains that is a mere approximation of this primordial and primal Will. This Will is almighty. Its forms are endless. It is no different from the *fire* of Heraclitus, a pervasive energy at play, inside all things, that seeks to order and reorder itself into ascending, uncanny objects. Its intent is mischievous, and beyond our ability to understand in words. In the life of organisms, this seeks to order itself into higher and more differentiated forms, that is, concretely, seeks the production of one supreme specimen. Peoples are nature's circuitous ways to great specimens and for this reason the peoples that have arisen out of nature must be preserved in their distinct forms. In same way see from all this that aesthetic physique has the most cosmic significance, and it is because of what I have said so far that aesthetic bodies are a "window to the other side," because they are the pinnacle of nature. The gods that surely exist but remain hidden have the most beautiful bodies we can imagine—they appeared to the ancient Greeks in dreams. Contrary to this exists the surfeit of flesh we see on the obese and in general the lassitude, the spiritual obesity, not only of modern life but of many historical forms of life as well, the domestic life of the village, of the village sewer, of the fetid valleys, of matriarchy and domestics, of slaves, the pollution of cities built on filth, the life of the swamp, the life of the human animal collapsed to mere life, life for the sake of life, as it devolves to the *yeast* form aesthetically, morally, intellectually, physically. On the other side is the life of the immortal gods who live in pure mountain air, and the sign of this life, where energy is marshaled to the production of higher order, is the aesthetic physique, the body in its glorious and divine beauty. What of the mind then? Well as rare as beautiful bodies are, the mind in the same condition is even more rare. Let us strive, in our decrepit, cancerous and fetid world, for what is concrete and what we can try to attain. Those who forget the body to pursue a "perfect mind" or "perfect soul" have no idea where to even start. Only physical beauty is the foundation for a true higher culture of the mind and spirit as well. Only sun and steel will show you the path.

16

Chimp in state of nature never jerks off, but in captivity he does, wat does this mean? In state of nature he's too busy, to put plainly. He is concerned with mastering space: solving problem of life in and under trees, mastering what tools he can, mastering social relations in the jockeying for power and status. Deprived of this drive to development and self-increase he devolves to pointless masturbation, in captivity, where he senses he is in owned space and therefore the futility of all his efforts and all his actions. The onanism of modern society is connected with its supposed "hyper-sexualization" and its infertility. It's not really hyper-sexualization, but the devolution of the spirit to the lassitude of a diffuse and *weak* sexuality. Life in owned space becomes drained of energy through low-grade pointless titillation—and nofap is a kind of cargo cult that tries to reestablish energy in order, on path of ascent. Sometimes, however, it's a successful cargo cult, but whether it works or no can be seen usually within a week. The unfortunate thing about all this is that w*m*n have exceptionally good antennae for this kind of thing, and when a man frees himself from these pressures...they *see* this from very far away. They have an instinct to seek out ascending life and drain it...they and the species thereby achieve their goals, but you are bled dry and sometimes left a husk. They revert life back to its irritated state, and by their drainage of vital essence they've laid low many great tasks.

17

I've always been attracted to filth and dirt, because something in me knew intuitively that it is only in the underseam of life as it exists today that you find the real "lacunae," the "holes" where *its reach* is limited or weak. I always sensed there was some real freedom in the blackest of red light districts among whores and junkies, perverts, and worse, with whom I've always chosen to take my dinners when I had the chance. I like the stories they told me, some showed letters from delusional Spanish engineer who wanted to marry her, another told me story of miscarriage her friend had in old pervert's bathroom, and how they flushed it down a toilet and then its name written on a piece of toilet paper. It's in this world and almost only in this world today that you can start to polish the claws nature gave you, assuming it gave you any. Unfortunately it's easy for a man with good antennae to see that even this world of shadows has at most a conditional existence. The truth is that *they* are allowing these "holes" because they, or the people who crafted the fabric in which the masters of lies operate, are smart enough to know you need these "free spaces": they are of great use to a manipulator. See how the Japanese, so famed for their love of law and order, have nevertheless always allowed the *yakuza* to operate running prostitution and meth rings and even worse. Such things have a serious function in Japanese society, as the mafia and other institutions have had in Western society. Only a cretinous government will get rid of such a world entirely, and thankfully we have very stupid governments in the West now. Their days are numbered. It is with sadness that you realize, eventually, after the first exhilarating rush of freedom in this world of the damned, that these spaces too, though not so pervasively "owned," have portals and gates manned by that which owns everything else. Still, it's better than nothing because in the moment all of that's still far away... on a late summer night when you are asked by corrupt lawyer to spy on Lebanese strip club owner and you're out in courtyard with 20-year-old prostie, she put cocaine on your tongue and you feel the ocean air at night fill you with the longing of the great sea.... you might almost forget suffocating air of gravity outside, and feel for a few minutes like animal before moment of hunt.

18

When speak of whoremoans you might think I'm a materialist reductionist, or am saying you are like machine. This is attitude of many scientists or maybe just cultists of science. Actually many on the left claim to have this attitude, though they can never explain what moral force their "rights" and "compassion" have, if it doesn't come from God or have some reality in human nature. When they say they are atheists, I never believe them: atheists act like Stalin or

Brezhnev, not like a Presbyterian schoolmarm. The truth is that these who make the core of the modern left are moral fanatics. There's not a drop of atheism or relativism in them. They don't enjoy the clear air of skepticism and never have. They always sneak in the soul or free will when you're not looking. They actually get off on this, and are acting out of spite, even spite against themselves. They want to feel they're not in control, "my hormones made me do it": what is this *you* apart from your hormones, your genes, your inborn instinct, then? "It's the genes," "it's the environment," "it's the economy or the oppression"—all versions of the *milieu* theory, a neurotic's theory according to Nietzsche. This is how they can also get themselves to believe in the transgender: these are people who believe that matter can somehow be corruptly configured, and that we all have disembodied souls with male or female essences. The whole attempt to redefine identity, not just sexual identity, as a matter of decision, meaning decision made arbitrarily, freely, a choice of the intellect or reason, is their desperate reach to find a new justification for the freedom of the will, the soul unrestrained by nature or biology. Such things make no sense when you realize you're your body and there's no you aside from this. The first lines of the *Iliad* make this clear: you do have a "soul" of sorts apart from your body...it just isn't you. It's a shade. It's completely homosexual.

19

Some think this view absolves you of your responsibility for your acts. But actually you're responsible for much more than your acts. That which is said to constrain or determine you biologically is actually what you are. *It* does restrain your acts according to its inherent ways of desiring and acting, but you *are* this it, and *it* decided to *be,* so actually you are responsible for much more, you're responsible for what you are. You are responsible for the good and bad things that happen to you, for any accident or disease you might experience! Actually it was all going to happen to you just the way it did at the moment of your birth or conception and even before, at the moment your parents had a glint for each other in the eye. There is fundamentally no difference between you and that glint.

20

Animals walk around in a state of permanent religious intoxication. This is the natural condition of the mind and intellect, the moment-to-moment perception, of man as well. I heard some computer fool say that religion is the "older virtual reality" experience, to justify his scam industry. No, the denuded state of the spirit and intellect, where you walk around "demystified" and "disenchanted" is the virtual reality condition, and a terrible condition at that. For the longest period of which we are at present aware, for hundreds of thousands of years in the Paleolithic, humans walked around, like healthy animal, in a state that we would today call religious delirium, but which is in fact the default state of all conscious and semi-conscious life. For long after the coming of civilization also, many continued in this condition, or did so during special times of the year or festivals where man could regain his free and natural state. It was civilization and in particular agricultural civilization that forbad this condition and plunged the majority of humans into a semi-permanent repressive or depressive frame. That this is consistent with, and even a prerequisite for, the impressive works and development of higher civilization and higher culture shouldn't be surprising: the majority of mankind suffered terribly also in their bodies from the coming of agriculture, the backbreaking labor, the malnourishment that shows itself in the smaller stature and more slender build of farmers' skeletors, of the destruction of their teeth, the atrophy of their brains and other organs. Agriculture allowed a steady food source, an increase in numbers, and above all the maintenance of an elite, free from these exactions, that lived parasitically on the many. But agriculture broke the human animal and domesticated him. Do you understand then what the "disenchanted" worldview *is?* I have to laugh at the "secular worldview," the disenchanted worldview, which is in fact the worldview or *mood* of the broken peasant farmer. "Science," supposedly the content....that's not even relevant here…

21

My favorite thing is to walk around the city during the day completely plastered, on very crowded streets or on boardwalk by sea or river, with container maybe it looks like iced tea or water but is full of alcohol. At night I don't enjoy as much, but during the day to walk around in a state of great enthusiasm and energy powered by liquor or, best of all, some kind of wine that energizes you to a great and holy rage. I don't mean really rage, because I'm laughing on the inside, but I love to walk around like this, to see the people, to accost strangers in all kinds of ways, nothing is more entertaining. I've often wondered at these times what it would be like, and how blessed life would be, if I could feel this way all the time and not just when I drink, and also never pay the price for it. Alcohol should never, by the way, be used for stress relief because after it crashes, and even the next day, there is a rise in cortisol so that unpleasant feelings become worse. But I wondered what it would be like to feel like this all the time and that there must be, or have been, people who do. Aren't we told this world is full of mutants? Why not a mutant who is perpetually full of this kind of euphoria…but even more, why not just one set of emotions, or one emotion. I've wondered at these times how life could be if you were possessed only by *one* specific feeling, and if there is a man who has only felt the purest and most intense anger, continually and nothing else, or who has felt only a very specific kind of joy and no other feeling…even sadness of certain kinds makes life beautiful and can be a spur to great things. Even panic is better than the numbness promoted in our time. What would a creature who only ever felt such a thing be like, and why can't one exist? It would be a monster, or a god, or in any case he would be possessed by a god.

22

Do you imagine that men of genius or, let's say, men of science in history walked around clear-headed, "disenchanted," *reasonable,* with the tight-assed attitude of the science cultist and materialist? No great discovery has ever been made by the power of reason. Reason is a means of communicating, imperfectly, some discoveries to others, and in the case of the sciences, a method of trying to render this communication certain and precise. But no one ever made a discovery through syllogisms, through reason, through this makeshift form of transmission. Great mathematicians *saw* spatial relations, as great physicists saw and to some extent *felt* physical relations. In contemplation of mathematical forms, there is almost a physical *feel* of geometric relations, and all mathematics at bottom is about geometric relations even when it doesn't seem so. Compare the Euclidian proof of the Pythagorean theorem, based on syllogism, which helps you understand nothing that's actually going on, with the imagistic proof of the three squares, that makes you perceive, physically perceive even in your body, why this theorem is true. Gauss, so beloved even by the tedious scientistic goblins that even Google gave him a cartoon, is famous to have said something like, "I got it...now I have to get it." Meaning, he had *seen* and felt the fundamental spatial relation he was searching, but now he had to translate it into the imperfect language of mathematics for others. Thus all mathematics and all science in general—mathematics is only the prototype and most precise of the sciences—is about the definitions, not about the proof, not about the process or—absurd!—the "algorithm." All great scientific discoveries, supposedly the great works of "reason," are in fact the result of intuitions and *sudden grasp* of ideas. And all such sudden grasp and reaching is based on what, in other circumstances, would be called a kind of religious intoxication: it depends on a state of the mind where the perceiving part of the intellect is absolutely focused, limpid, yet driven by the most relentless energy, an energy to *penetrate.* Direct perception is already "intellectualized" and in fact much closer to the innate "intelligence" of things than cerebral syllogisms. No scientist worth anything has ever felt pride at using algorithms or trial-and-error to solve a problem. Yes, feminists are right that "science" is patriarchal in this sense, that it is a "rape" of nature. Real scientists like Galois are monsters of will, and the preponderance of men in the hard sciences is explained by this orientation of character, as also by the fact that the minds of men more than of women are capable of sustained focus on one thing (women are better at multitasking). There are women who were great scientists, but, like women who were great chess players, or poets, they are probably spiritual lesbians.

23

The modern peasant just replaces the artificial prejudices of superstitions and village old wives' tales with the superstitions of science, which he receives ready-made from authorities among the popularizers of science. He loves them because of the creature comforts he believes they provide through technology. He is a cargo cultist—he knows nothing of what goes into the discoveries of science, nor the way the substance is transmitted among scientists, he just has a propagandized image of some of the results. This is no different from belief in Big Magic, which is how many primitives think of science—the Big Magic of the white man. It's not even the substance of science that is the problem because it could be of great use, as much as any other popular religion has been: the problem is the frame of spirit that it puts the acolyte in. It makes him think he has power over the processes of nature which are at present actually very poorly understood. By removing primal fear—the only kind of awe that drives the many—it injects a toxic mix of complacency, arrogance, brutality, fanaticism that is all just under the surface only so long as times are good. Science as popular religion brings no true consolation but instead feeds a kind of false pride, pride in spiting oneself—does this sound familiar? It should sound familiar to women most of all. It actually makes the many more servile to the authorities who are presumed to understand and manipulate the technology. That is its purpose, to make the many submit, which wouldn't be bad, if they weren't submitting to the lords of lies. You can see from all this anyway why Enlightenment can never happen but also why those critics of Enlightenment like most of the followers of Heidegger go the wrong way. They are right when they say, in so many words, that the inborn character of every man is in some way unique, the biology too particular, much more so than the more uniform character of animals. For animals the worker ant, or two fruitflies, will have exactly the same inborn, but humans are all slightly different. From this they draw the conclusion that no common "way" can suffice for all, but that the only authentic way for you can come from the needs of your inner self. Every adherence to an external code, religion, or ideology is "inauthentic" and represents essentially a form of mind control, your adopting the thoughts of another, inappropriate for your own metabolism, biology, peculiar conditions for growth or flourishing. Yes, it is true, Nietzsche went so far as to avoid reading anything written by others, so as not to infect his mind! And he was a mutant with a very particular biology—such types often are, and he was right that for them, physiology, diet, may be the most pressing research necessary. But he never forgot that the fundamental fact of nature is inequality, and this is something these people, the followers of Heidegger, and Heidegger himself to a great degree, all forget. It is madness to ask the common prefab run of man to fashion his own way, his own "religion"—the many find solace and meaning only in submission. It is good that this is so, and they shouldn't be made to feel ashamed for it. So much of the modern idiocy is based on shaming those who would find true pleasure in submission! The long chain of being is held together by command and obedience. The many are not so different from one another, nor their conditions of life so different. In the end you too, no matter how special or a genius you may be, are held together to the average man through many ties of biology, so that you would both do well to pay attention to what is common, especially insofar as the body is concerned. The body is not a private thing: the "individual" body is likely diseased. The universal body, the correct type discovered by ancient Greek science and art, is not something you will develop by nurturing your own "individual" quirks, doxies and faggotries. Biology works according to types and grades of manifestation, not according to the development of "unique" personal eccentricities. Science rightly understood helps us understand the types, the species, the true cleavages of nature. Science is not in and of itself the cause of our problems, of your "alienation," nor does it have any content beyond who uses it and for what. Science is a great tool because it can uncover for us the biological conditions of all life and the relationships between types of life. It can, as Nietzsche predicted, settle the question of the true hierarchy of values, or more precisely, the real ladder of life, the true hierarchy of biological types. What prevents this from happening is not inherent to science or technology as such. It is a political and sociological problem—one way or another, in time, the right force will take hold of the power of science and reveal its true potential. Science was never meant to be for comfort!

24

I don't talk about if God exists, I don't know this. I've never had any feeling for this one way or another. I've sat in houses of religions, but I always felt nothing, it put me to sleep. Even the novelty of a Buddhist or Hindu temple wore off very fast: I enjoyed the spectacle but could tell...these priests are just more piledrivers. I was always so bored. How can the secret and hidden and precious things be about *doctrine* and just more *talking?* But—and I don't know why people put these things together, because for me they never had anything to do with each other—even as a small boy I felt every object was inhabited by an uncanny shadow or spirit. I paid honor to certain toys and certain objects I found outside and hid carefully. No one ever taught me to do this. I found dead animal and buried it with ceremony. I always felt I could talk to animal and that they were my brothers and sisters. This "animism" is the natural religion of man, and shows itself even to small child left alone to play. I remember fondly a small white dog under thickets of wisteria bushes growing on corrugated steel, and I believe this dog has followed me in different forms my whole life. But I'm almost sure that gods exist, and in any case, the argument against the one God isn't the same as against the other gods. In all the fulminations of Sam Harris, and Hitchens, and the "new atheists," there's nothing really new—they want to banish not just religion from public life, but to enter your own mind and replace whatever vestiges of old organized religions are there with their own very stupid organized religion. If they have an easy time of it, this is because monotheism overreached. It made such grand claims... and when these claims were abandoned it left people with the impression that there really is nothing besides "science," which of course, nobody really understands, because it's nothing but a method. It would have been far more honest to embrace skepticism but of course *they* would never let you take the logical conclusion. But still, forget for a moment all the claims made about God, about the creation of matter out of nothing—which runs against all intuition and all observation that you can make yourself...you don't even need science for that. Paglia said once that the real novelty of the one God was that he spoke the world into existence. How different this was from all other creation myths! All pagans knew the world was eternal, and that its present condition was a result of cycles of birth, rebirth, regeneration, copulation: the Japanese even have myths about gods shitting on fields to make them fertile! How proper, it makes many other things about Japanese culture easier to understand. Monotheism, even of the intellectual or deist variety, and especially that variety, makes all kinds of claims too about the lawfulness of matter or of nature, about intelligent design and the like. It's actually much closer to the science that claims to disprove it, than to the original paganism of all mankind. So much of this story makes time a line and makes matter conditional on a deity or creator that lives outside it: the creation of matter out of nothing, the creation of your soul out of nothing. Matter is dead, in some ways homogenous, and its meaning is "divine" only in the sense that it reveals the creation of the external deity, or even better, just the laws he made to govern it. It seems and feels wrong, or runs against the immediate perception of the world, so it requires *faith,* a concept unknown to ancient pagans of all kinds. For this reason the Romans considered Christians and Jews to be no different from atheists. That view is very different. As such, there is no "scientific" reason why you would have to rule out the existence of beings stronger, superior, more intelligent, more magnificent than us, equipped with powers that appear magical to our understanding. The only reason I can think to dismiss this is Schopenhauer's, his amusing refutation of God—that any being of intelligence higher than man's would have already abolished itself long ago. But if you don't believe that, what reason can there be? Please no say "there no proof," "I didn't see it." Scientific proof would be totally forbidden here: in fact there are many strange occurrences that have been recorded by many, as much as any event can be recorded, but this lacks any scientific meaning, it's a case of "not applicable." If an impish deity of the lower kind, with which the world is full, some purple goblin with a wicked face showed itself to a pedant in a white coat, the scientist would convince himself he was hallucinating—and in any case, without being available for study, for testing, for experiments that can be seen by others (this standard has been abandoned for many fields lately), its existence would not fall within the power of "science" at all. No, and what do you say to ancient accounts that such creatures showed themselves to men before, and maybe still do? Why would they show themselves to you? The weakness and spinelessness of modern man—no god would show himself to such creatures, to be jeered at! Why? Remember why the young men in Mishima's story of the League of the Divine Wind were so inflamed with passion and anger on behalf of the immortal gods. They knew that, without them, without the breed of warriors, the many would forget the gods. They would become powerless spirits hiding among the reeds, the subject of superstition, ridicule. The true gods have a kind of power, but not the kind the many imagine. Why should they care for mankind? They are rare and precious, and it is for man to find, acknowledge, and honor them. This, at least, was the ancient view: and the foundation and preservation of *oracles* was the first question of life and also of statecraft. Gods could not control nature or fate, but could reveal its workings at key times. If a god showed himself today to you, in a dream, would you have the inner energy and power to honor him and do his bidding in the world? Or would you, neutered by the modern pervasive hivemind of the slave, dismiss it, and yourself as unreal or unworthy, when it is the modern bugman and his blabbering that lacks reality. But I want you to be intoxicated with the highest enthusiasm and ready to receive these greatest blessings with great confidence!

25

Nerds, so prized by the middlebrow clothmos who rule the cities and want to think that, well, at least they're *smart and deserve RESPECT*, are people who possess a kind of self-destructive parody of intelligence. Their facility with pointless concepts and abstractions make them think they have an understanding of real things when all they have is a misunderstanding of words and grammar, overgeneralized to the point of meaninglessness.

Simple people confuse a facility with words for real intellect. It would be very easy to speculate, for example, on the two forms of life I mentioned above and to say, as some do, that there is a progress in the universe from the simple to the more complex. This is similar to those who believe in historical progress, and that there is a motion in history to greater reasonableness, or peace, or prosperity, or freedom, whatever. All of this way of thinking is wrong. While I believe the two physiological processes I mentioned do describe two different kinds of life, and their differing conditions and aims, there is no evidence for any motion in time in favor of one or the other, either when we consider the universe or just human history. If anything, the evidence is motion toward the lower forms of life. I have no doubt anyway that beings of magnificent beauty and complexity existed before, but disappeared because the conditions for their preservation were that much more difficult. No doubt also that human civilization came and went in many cycles, over many hundreds of thousands of years. Civilizations far more advanced than ours are buried under miles of ash and rock, or under the ice of Antarctica, or were entirely pulverized. The memory of such things comes to very sensitive youths with a nervous system so strong that, as a parasite, it takes over the organism: in moments of limpid calm, a small perturbation in the will brings a faint feeling of a memory from long ago...they suddenly remember, like a revelation...

26

Reincarnation is the original belief of every society or tribe that drew its conclusions from observation of life and nature. The new religions, the faith of Israel and those that have come from it, and many others that came about at that time, or have arisen since—I believe Zoroastrianism is likely the root also of the faith in the Bible—have some divine inspiration at their beginnings, but I believe at least the way they are interpreted now is a design of the human mind, and calculated. They are abstract, utilitarian, and crudely political. Before this nearly every society had a belief in reincarnation. This still has remained in some places, although the moral meaning imposed on reincarnation by Buddhism and Hinduism is, like Plato's, for reasons of social utility and is political. But there is much significance in the primitive belief in reincarnation, which is more like a primal and perennial belief. It is universal and naïve, and I believe therefore it must have some truth. It's not possible to dismiss it as wish-fulfillment, and a false desire for immortality: first, because as we see, the later religions achieve this in a much better way with the teaching of the afterlife, but most of all because to many people, reincarnation is a kind of hell. You've all had very comfortable lives and maybe wouldn't mind reliving something like this again, but try to visit a burn ward. Life is so painful for so many that suicide, an escape from this infernal prison, is very common at all times. But, unfortunately for the suicides, that death is not the end of the story. I believe reincarnation is fundamentally true, even though most of these religions taught it in a metaphorical and popular form called metempsychosis. This is the belief that the soul, the supposed (but false) unity of will and intellect, is fully reborn. This is false. The intellect is a merely physical quality like muscular strength and can't be "reborn" any more than your muscles are literally reborn. You are not at bottom your intellect, this is impossible, although this is the assumption of almost all modern people even when they claim otherwise. They pay lip service to "supremacy of the desires," or to biological determinism, but they still believe they are their intellects, just imprisoned by flesh and matter and genes and a biological "programming." This is wrong! And it's not the intellect that is reborn, I will tell you what is. Take a fruitfly, or a worker ant. This type of being is very close to plant-life in some ways. It has very primitive intellect, very primitive nervous system. There are inborn ways of behaving, of reacting to certain stimuli, inborn desires and orientations "in the blood," and when you kill one ant, the next one over will be identical in this regard. Its rebirth is "instantaneous" because the ant has a will that is shared uniformly across its type in the hive, and is therefore persistent and enduring. Once the queen dies, the next queen is indistinguishable from it in that thing that Schopenhauer calls the will, what he says is inborn way of wanting, and is in a very literal sense a "reincarnation" of this same thing. If you don't see this it's because you keep confusing yourself for your intellect. But that part of you that is really you persists even when your intellect is asleep, and would persist even if you experienced total amnesia. If you doubt, just ask yourself... someone you love, if you had to choose—would you rather they forgot everything but still behaved the way you always knew they did, or would you rather that they kept all their memories and knowledge but had a radical change in personality? This question is easy to answer...if you love someone only for what they know or remember...everyone knows this is a betrayal because that's not *who you are*. And in fact there's no such thing as a radical change in personality. The lower forms of life are nearly uniform in their wills or inborn ways of acting, and also very simple: in the case of amoeba, yeast, and such they are not far removed from the behavior of the natural forces, like gravity, which is completely uniform and persistent. Once dead, they are immediately reborn, and indeed live simultaneously in numerous bodies. For higher and more differentiated animals, the Will appears more particularly defined for each type, species, and finally each specimen when it comes to the human. But this biological reality, independent of what is known, remembered, or consciously decided, is a matter of the blood and body, and this same being, thing, or Will, call it what you will, will be reborn in just the same way. In a different time, but this same particular way of desiring and behaving that is inside you will come again: this is the real meaning of reincarnation. And with the glut of humans in our time, we have to wonder if the same being also lives now in multiple bodies sometimes. Where do these beings come from? Some have said that these new billions of hue-mans, that in a previous life they must have been yeast, amoeba, locusts and other insects that are born in multitudes in each season. I'd like this to be true, but I think rather that in previous ages mankind also swelled to many billions or even more ...and also I have no doubt the entire universe is teeming with life of all kinds.

27

It would be interesting to know what the "extinction" event or path is in each previous human cycle of civilization. If it is something completely random and external, like asteroids or volcanoes, or if it is something inherent to civilization as such...some circumstance or behavior that leads to virulent disease, or some kind of great weapon or maybe even something more uncanny. I wonder if the peoples and religions that exist now also existed in past cycles under different names with slightly different superficial circumstances and appearances, but in all fundamental ways otherwise the same. And if one or a set of these, or some new belief that hasn't even appeared yet, is the cause of the end of civilization in every cycle. A frog once suggested to me that the explosion of African populations in our time is the event that the movie *Alien* describes, a population bred under the most extreme pathogenic load, and that, despite its weaknesses in cold weather, can nevertheless wreak so much damage on the rest of the world that societies collapse under the march of the *zombi* ...I personally doubt this. Asia will shut them out without glancing twice or hearing of their suffering. I think instead the end in previous cycles has varied but that very often, and most interesting, one cause has been the emergence of brotherhoods of savage men who have decided to purify the earth and rid it of the infestation of the human-cockroach. Because unfortunately in the long run the development of civilization and comfort leads to the proliferation of damaged life, the innovation of mankind leads to unspeakable abortions of life, and men on the periphery who want to preserve the natural order begin to plot the end of everything. I also wonder if some ancient civilization has managed to escape all these cycles of destruction and has hidden underground somewhere. Maybe they are really eternal and live life as an experiment, detached, seeing it as a playful dream they can observe at a distance…maybe an emissary surfaces from time to time so they can amuse themselves. I shudder to think, though, that by this same reasoning the aborted robot life to which the mass of mankind inevitably degenerates in each cycle of civilization also survived, maybe in small communities of "moles," inside dry hills of limestone, or not far underground in old networks of caves and tunnels. No doubt stories of vampires, kobold, cryptid humanoids and many others might refer to these degenerated stragglers that prey on us and terrorize us….no doubt many among the ranks of deities have come from both types, and stranger things still exist under the earth. Please see DEROs if interested. There are more things….

28

There can be no "artificial intelligence" in the way that people really mean it. If they mean some machine that approximates the intellect of man, this may be possible, and even very useful, although they're very far from their goals at the moment. Success at chess is their one great achievement, but they fail still at kicking a ball, pouring ketchup, recognizing simple objects …could one hunt, or survive being hunted? But they never mean just the intellect in this way, or a crude approximation of it: when people speak of "artificial intelligence" what they always mean is artificial *life*, a robot of some kind, or an artificial consciousness indistinguishable from human consciousness. There is an apparently different but in fact similar speculation that nerds love: that the universe is "logic" or information. That what constitutes matter can in fact be recorded as "information," as relations of logic, and that therefore the universe must be precisely this—this is behind also the belief that you can "upload" your intelligence to a computer and attain immortality, and many related forms of imbecility. The motivation for this is nerdishness and also somewhat the Jewish way of thinking, or the Judaizing tendency that promotes facility with words and number, but approaches mental deficiency and even retardation when it comes to anything visual. The Jewish hatred of matter, an ancient prejudice that precedes the Bible, and the hatred also for beauty that they share with other Semitic peoples—and many others besides—all of this comes together to promote this kind of aggressive nerdishness. This is the origin of many of these claims, though it shouldn't be imagined that here or elsewhere I am referring to all Jews, or that this absolves non-Jews. Because the "Judaizing" tendency I talk about is inherent to human nature, and is very common also among non-Jews, and in some degree it exists within everyone, together with the counter-acting love of vibrant matter, image, and beauty. It just exists in different degrees in different people, and peoples. In any case, all of these delusions, that *you* can be "uploaded" because your "brain" can be uploaded, that "the universe is information" or that something like "artificial intelligence" actually can exist, are all at bottom the same delusion and the same power fantasy of the nerd. The nerd can be described as a person of inelegant and pedantic intelligence, often middling intelligence, who takes excessive pride in the intellect, even in the memorization of facts, the design of clumsy concepts to which reality is then expected to fit like to bed of Procrustes.... And he identifies with it. There are very rare people in history, even a few saints and martyrs, who were ashamed of their evil character and will, and sought salvation in contemplation, sought some escape in this. These are sometimes noble people, but this doesn't describe the nerd. The nerd doesn't hate himself, his nature, his tendencies or spirit, nor is his intellect powerful enough to over-awe his needling will and consider things without the pressure of interest or the gravity of petty desires. He never sees things like the true genius or the artist does, when the perceiving part of the intellect becomes so powerful that it really overpowers everything else...so that the fullness of the object occupies all of consciousness and an idea, or some new insight into the world, is actually grasped. No, the nerd is a creature of will, under the direction of a petty will in the everyday sense, and all of his thoughts, concepts, and designs have a *forced* quality because they refer always to need and desire for some kind of gain. This very often is just material gain, but the desire for prestige is even worse. In men of intellect the desire for prestige is often the most disgusting, especially when there's no native manliness, because this leads to cowardice and lies, to others and oneself. For this reason Nietzsche said manliness is the first requirement of the philosopher, but there's no one farther from the philosopher than the unmanly nerd, and there's no enemy more implacable of the human race and of the genius of the species, than just this nerd and everything he represents. The attempt to "mimic" life through algorithms, through the brute-force of trial-and-error, will never create either life or "consciousness"—just what would such a machine be "conscious" of?—but just that, a mimicry or parody of the middling human intellect. A mirror and exaltation of the false intellect of the nerd, that never leaves the stream of words, syllogisms, motives and desire, that is always forced and contrived, because it's under pressure of some petty need. And it's really grotesque. It's as if you have a girl you desire, she dies but using Big Magic you reanimate her corpse, put makeup on her, re-teach this *zombi* to speak, force her to copy all of her old habits, condition her like you would a pigeon to act in ways you remember and that you liked. But in the end she's just a reanimated live-action doll, and this is grotesque. This is just what "AI" is. It is a fantasy of power of the conspiracy of biological interests that unites the nerds, the intellect of "reason"—the party that believes in empty words—the middling, and the Jews of the human spirit into hoping for their *golem*. "AI" is the *golem* of those who hate *life*.... It is their true Messiah and their vengeance.

29

Youth and beauty are universally hated in almost all human societies in history. These societies are run by decrepit, sclerotic old men. Sometimes they use image of fat woman "Earth Mother" to beat the young men over the head with and make them submit. Other times they promote ugliness in all ways: ugliness and perversity in custom, scarification, circumcision, self-mutilation. Customs and religious authorities that concern themselves with how you should wipe your ass, brush teeth, how many fingers to insert in anus to achieve such and such "magical-medical" goal, petty legalisms of all kinds—the Shiite sect among Muslims and rabbinical Judaism are most like this. All of this smothers genuine religious enthusiasm and the true oracular science, from which can evolve arts of great beauty. Often their food is unappetizing and looks like boiled rocks. Their languages—most human languages are so hard to listen to! Tagalog is almost torture to hear, though I don't mean to single out this culture, it's hardly the worst in terms of love of ugliness (actually the Filipinos can be a pleasant people with an impish sense of humor inherited from the long-lost *negritos* now absorbed in their population). Their people are ugly: millennia of arranged marriages, for financial gain, among the Indians—originally a noble people—led to a nation now, of one billion, that almost never wins any athletic contests, that has won fewer gold medals since its inception than tiny Croatia has since 1992, where both the men and the women are inbred, ugly, unsexy, and almost deformed. I don't mean to pick on them, because they're hardly the only ones, and this ugliness, physical ugliness, is almost universal in the human race. Beauty is the very rare and precious preserve of tribes that have striven to promote child-making for something other than financial, social and political gain. No, the promotion of ugliness is nearly universal and the love of beauty is so rare: among the great civilizations, only the ancient Greeks, the French, the Japanese, and somewhat the Italians are true lovers of beauty and refinement, and have based their existence exclusively on the promotion of beauty. How many times in history have cultures become ugly and petty because financial interest overrode eugenics in marriage—and free love, though not perfect, is somewhat more eugenic than letting fathers trade daughters for personal gain. In their hatred and distrust of beauty one feels such societies live under a tremendous *pressure* of needs. Their true ruler is the god of gravity and they are dominated by fears of the future, unspeakable anxieties about money and matter, and importune, brutish behaviors all motivated by *need,* by the desire to *grasp,* by the feeling they all nourish that *they're being taken advantage of.* They always feel they're being *disrespected.* The desire for *respect* is the true mark of the forever-slighted. The distrust of beauty is sometimes sold as the high-minded rejection of material desire by the saintly or the kind or the contemplative. But that's just nonsense, and you can see it in this way. Beauty-hating cultures have one other peculiarity they all share, which is very revealing. They hate also privacy and personal space, they hate also beauty in good and refined manners. These societies are based on such popular solidarity that it's considered normal to barge in on other people, absurd to demand to knock; they make animal sounds when eating—or, the way such people are often said to *smell* in history whenever such societies are encountered—all of this tells you what the hatred of beauty is really about. Freud refers to the inner pain many of his clients experienced trying to shift from this kind of medieval, collective, smothering culture of ugliness to one where personal space and distance, refinement and beauty, were instead valued. It's about the hatred of distinction or superiority, hatred of the principle of *difference and distance* between individuals, that is by contrast so prized in those very few beauty-loving cultures. And the hatred of superiority comes from the suspicion the many in such beauty-hating societies feel, that, in not being subject to the horrible pressures of *need* and anxiety under which they themselves live, that the beautiful and carefree make a mockery of what they take most seriously. The beautiful threaten to unravel the regimentation under which they must subject their constant crude *need* for things. This is why such societies descend to the lowest types of faggotry whenever their native laws are even slightly relaxed. Islam is most like this. Jews, when devoid of their religion, as well as Persians who live under the tyranny of Shiite law, and most of all the people of the Gulf States, all revert to a crude animal condition without their rigid laws and become completely dissolute, as the Arabs were said to have been before Islam. And they will soon return to this. I don't need to add notes for spergs and pedants: men like John Milius are excepted from such judgments, but their existence has nothing to do one way or another with my point here, which is about general types and the ways these generate. I am speaking of two opposing views of life that are based in two very different needs of two very different biological orientations. There can be no compromise between those who live under the pressure of *need* and of material increase, who are the walking shadows of the dead, and on the other side, those who are carefree, joyous, pleasure-loving and worship beauty. One seeks the preservation and expansion of mere life, the other seeks the exaltation of life.

30

Among the Greeks the man of power was called *aner,* who was different from the other word used, *anthropos,* which referred just to some shadow-being, indistinct, some kind of humanoid shape. The real man was rare, and most males were not and are not real men! The word in beginning was used only for demigods and superhumans like Achilles or Diomedes or Odysseus. In the *Iliad* Diomedes in his moment of glory is compared to lion whose spirit has been aroused by anger at wound, and scatters the shepherds and dogs before him. Athena kindled a fire on his head and shoulders and marked him as one possessed by the true inner force inside all things. This burst out of him now and made itself light up above all others. The real man was a man filled by courage and daring that all came from an excess of being. This idea was shared also by other Aryan cultures; the Roman *vir,* the Sanskrit and Avestan *nar,* the Welsh *ner,* the Proto-Indo-European *Hner* all ultimately refer to a kind of vital life-force capable of superhuman strength. There is other word, related, having to do with manly youth: *ayu; ayu* refers to the youthful life-force that renews itself in each generation, that moves from life to life without end, forever persisting. It is behind all the Indo-European words for youth, and youthful strength and power. It appears in Latin *iuuenis,* in Sanskrit, and all the Germanic and English forms. But most of all it is this same word, this same idea that is behind the Latin *aetas* and *aeternus,* behind the vision of an age, a cyclical age, of eternity. How pregnant in meaning that youth and eternity are the same word and idea in these languages! The Gothic and Germanic words are the same. This idea very vivid in Greek! In this the words *aiei,* meaning forever, and the word *aion,* both contain at their root this meaning: of life-span, life-force, youthful strength. These peoples saw the vigor of youth as the true driving force behind life and behind all things, forever renewing itself, reincarnating itself anew in each generation in full force, though the memories of men and of societies may disappear. If you want the most beautiful poetic expression of this view, you must see in the *Iliad* when Homer describes the death of Euphorbus. His death is compared to young tree in its prime blown down by strong wind. Pythagoras, looking on Euphorbus' shield in Sicily, broke into tears, remembering that he had been this man. He knew of what was hidden on the other side of the shield. This view persists: and this is why someone like D.H. Lawrence could look on the sarcophagi of the ancient Tuscans and see in this pleasure- and beauty-loving people a celebration of something very similar. They put on their funerary objects images of reveling, and feasting, and abundant flourishing life and great joy, wine parties, leaping dolphins, to remind themselves that this irrepressible force, nature, *youth* continues anew in each generation and is never defeated by death. In same way when I poast physiques of beautiful and handsome youths I do so because in contemplating them I am filled with a deep calm and joy—I see in them the persistent rejuvenation of this same eternal force, that is inside all things. I see in this force the hidden design and intention of nature, its reaching beyond itself. Its designs are unspeakable and what it reaches and wants is mysterious to us, can only be understood imperfectly and through metaphor. Its "plan" and design is beyond human comprehension, but it is without doubt that *it* is striving, against numerous other "factions" and centrifugal forces, for the production and creation of a superior creature of some kind, a specimen of terrible beauty and power. I have no doubt that the gods, if they exist, would look only like perfected and improved versions of beautiful physiques of young men, just like they showed themselves to the Greek oracles in dreams. They were the first to discover the true biological and physical form of the man, the correct form, the true proportions. I have no doubt also that this force, in being *inside* us together with others, has made human history, life, and our own minds the battleground and stage of its action, and that passivity in the face of its power is therefore absurd: it calls on us to allow ourselves to be possessed by it, and to wage war on its behalf against its enemies. If you want to understand the true power of *aion,* of the eternal youthful energy that is the universe, you must study what remains from Heraclitus when he uses this word, and how he connects it to the idea of *fire* that is the essence of all things and all action. And he is very right when he says, "The best desire one thing above all, ever-flowing eternal fame among mortals; but the many glut themselves like cattle." *This* is what I believe in!

Part Two: Parable of Iron Prison

31

If you recognize pathology, brokenness, denatured life as what it is, it can teach you a lot about life in healthy state. There is nothing wrong with looking in life under distress, if you no confuse it for life in ascent and freedom. When you put some kind of working dog, like terrier, even cute Jack Russell in city apartment, they will start to try to dig through the floor. This mode is inborn to them, they seek the development of their powers, and there are very few sadder things than to see animal thwarted like this. Playing at becoming itself, but reduced to a doll and useless acting. Carl Schmitt said, "They've put us out to pasture." This is the condition of life in modern world.

32

Modern world not bad just because modern; and it is better than some ages in the past. Many parts of past were as bad, or worse, than our situation, and for the same reasons. The modern is "nothing new": it is the return of a very ancient subjection and brokenness under new branding, promoted by new concepts and justifications. If you want to see our future look to Europe as it existed before 1600 BC, or much of the world as it was until recently and still is....the communal life of the longhouse with its young men dominated and broken by the old and sclerotic, by the matriarchs, the blob and yeast mode in human life overtaking and subjecting all higher aspiration. Aztec "cities" with twenty morons sleeping and eating off the floor, demagogued in the masses by blood-hungry priests with dead eyes. It is no different if they use the doxies of Reason and Logos to cart us off to this life.

33

A history of modern brokenness—So many different things have been written about the evils of modernity, or the crisis of our situation. Both on left and right many, maybe most, feel something has gone terribly wrong. Even those who love some aspects of the new age, like technology, look away from our banal time and instead hope for a futuristic flourishing that is not yet here. I'm a little tired of all this! I don't want to just repeat more aspersions of modernity, which many of you already know. Most of these are footnotes or commentaries to Nietzsche's Prologue from *Zarathustra*, where he describes the Last Man. The Last Man has been wrongly confused for the bourgeois, though Nietzsche says it's something much worse. Houellebecq, whose explanations of the sexual problem of modernity, of the *incel* —all of these explanations are amazing and true, but even he is just following Nietzsche. If you want to understand true problem of our time, you can read that, then, and I won't dwell on it. I want only to deal with one particular case of domestication, brokenness, of potentially high life that has been thwarted, to illustrate modern problem. The peculiar "history" of how the *queen* develops, the modern effeminate homosexual, is very telling. The problem of the modern homosexual is revealing because it is the model according to which many other kinds of higher life have been thwarted and warped into something else. Don't be fooled by propagandists: the modern homo has nothing to do with ancient "predatory bisexuality" or with the pederastic rites found in many societies. On one hand such people as the modern *queen* have always existed but on the other, there are many specimens now who become this, who would not have before. It is very unfortunate event in life of animal. Camille Paglia says that the modern homosexual is the product of the pressures of post-industrial life. Her model for this is that a very sensitive young boy, open to aesthetic experience of all kinds, maybe the kind of slightly neurotic and artistic boy that a century ago would have experienced synaesthesia; such boy is turned off by the horseplay and "rough" masculinity of his brothers and father and other boys his age. The distancing from this masculinity is concurrent with his becoming over-close with his mother, idolizing the feminine: upon puberty, the distance or fear from masculinity leads him to eroticize it, while he turns away from women, either because of too much familiarity, or too much awe. In this she is only half right, and the other half of the story I discovered from an alien mind whose teachings have been spread among some of the frogs. His name Harro MJ, but I think this is false name. I tell some of his ideas here as best I understood. He tells I believe his own story, or someone he knows: he tells of how modern world corrupted his nature through stricture and turned him into a homo. But I think his story speaks to many others, who didn't turn into ghey, but who have nevertheless been disfigured in some other way... by the same force. Now, Paglia's restatement of Freud is correct, but she misses an important element of the story, which is why such a boy turns away from the masculinity of his peers in the first place. It is not horseplay or the roughness of male competition as such that makes him turn away, but the utterly fake or artificial character of such displays, usually, in our time. Such boy perceives what his peers don't, the conditional and entirely *dependent* character of life in our age. It is not the masculinity, the competition for status among men, the physical roughness, that makes him turn away... but the fact that all such play is happening in already *owned space.* It is this aspect of our time that is crucial to understand. When I speak of something like owned space, it must not remain mere word. When you understand something: I mean you must see and feel it like you would a landscape you know from youth, how to navigate all its nooks, the different heights of earth, the banks of streams, where the trees are and how it feels inside them, how long it takes walking from this or that group of beech to the abandoned factory, so that the map is already in your body. This is only way to really understand something. I believe boy like this is one of the types that sees through the charade the lords of lies have dangled in front, the shadow-play to dazzle the many, and he is turned off, maybe not by manliness, but the buffoonish, deluded character of modern masculinity. The defeated male that is turned into a peon and a neutered beast for women and hidden masters is a terrible thing to see. The jockeying for status, the physical fights, the adventures boys are supposed to have in a state of nature...all of this is in nature meant as preparation for life, for a life of conquest and expansion. Roman teenagers of patrician class were sent already on missions on behalf of Empire abroad. Modern adult

Western male seeks permission to watch other men playing sports, quaff vegetable oil relish, beg for "coochie" in simulated intercourse, masturbation with plastic on dick. Precisely a character born for conquest, for expansion, a precocious type of boy who seeks *real* development and the real domination of the space around him, who understands in his blood that play and manliness are *to this end,* precisely such a boy will have his expectations about life crushed and thwarted as soon as his eyes open. This may be around the age of six or seven, but it sometimes happens earlier. Such boy then comes to have only contempt for those among his peers who, not seeing the subjection we are in, continue under their delusion and *accept* the breaking that the lords of shadows begin on the human spirit around this age of awakening—by nine or ten, the "education" is almost already complete in our time. They submit to the yoke and their sham simulated masculinity is now a parody of the true manliness, which in a state of ascent develops into the will to actually dominate space around oneself, not into a caricature for the benefit of women. But this domination is not possible when *space is already owned.* This intuition of *owned space* comes on one very early: with eyes open, it's like an evil spirit inhabits everything. I think there are many types of energetic and perceiving boys who reach this stage, who are turned off by the moral and biological self-castration of their conventional peers, who sense the suffocating limitations of modern space. The rest of this story is more particular to the boy who as response becomes a homo or trap, and Paglia is right about that part—masculinity rejected simply because of distance from other boys in general, mostly as a result of a certain native over-sensitivity. But then there is the added observation that when, late in adolescence or some time in youth, such boy decides he is "gay," that is but the final act of self-misunderstanding. The drama of his spirit is reinterpreted on sexual terms. He has convinced himself that the feeling of suppression and dread that had accompanied him his whole life was because his sexual desires or "sexuality" had been repressed by "society." He forgets how these sexual desires developed in the first place, that these desires themselves were a circuitous result of the truth that dawned on him in silence, the truth of the utter subjection and domestication of the space in which he found himself. In becoming "gay" he believes he is escaping that sense of primal limitation and subjection that he felt as a small boy: he has reinterpreted his entire drama as a maudlin story of sexuality suppressed or oppressed by retrograde social and political norms. In this he becomes an unwitting pawn himself of the very power that as a young boy he had intuited to be the enemy, the great and suffocating shadow of our time, that smothers all higher life out. The gay is the spiritual foot-soldier of the new regime, when he is born to be its enemy. This is the unusual part of this realization, that some of the most sensitive and perceptive youths, those maybe imbued with spark of inspiration and a conquering, expanding spirit, end up becoming the vanguard of that which has smothered and broken them. In a previous age they wouldn't have been gay at all in the first place. The story of such boy is story of all higher types in our time. Not all gays are of this origin—there is Jeffrey Dahmer, there are others. And of course not all higher types become gay, only a tiny minority. But all higher types in our age are afflicted by a similar drama of the spirit—what happens later, the sexualization of this alienation particular to this case, I use only as the most vivid example. Now in all this you see this idea of space or territory that is already closed and owned. And this brings up the question of who or what this force is. I think the answer to this problem isn't so simple, but one feature of this new condition in modern age is that the masters are hidden. That is even why this condition of subjection seems so suffocating, because *they hide,* and so there is no opportunity for open and manly challenge. This problem is then to be understood through example of a different type...and I mean that of the *spook.* Vivid and instructive is the matter of the *gay underworld,* which no longer really exists in our time. But in the 1950's and a little before then, when the system of global tyranny was being firmly erected, it should not be a surprise from everything that has been said, that the gay underworld was the "negative" of the new world order, its sieve and pressure valve. *The gay underworld was part of "the remainder."* The phenomenon of "homosexuality" in the modern world reaches up to the most profound of political and social problem: it was always the ghost world, the underworld left over that the engineers of our time couldn't manage or account for in the erection of the Leviathan. This underworld included far more than the gays of that time, of course: that's the point. But the gays formed a kind of "bulk population" that allowed an easy bridge between this world and ours. They made it far more permeable to others as well: if you had girlfriend, maybe artsy girlfriend, she had ghey friend; you could go with them to lounge of this half-world, and there would be there...maybe two social contacts removed...there would...one of *them.*

68

But now that this world has disappeared, you have no easy way of even knowing where to start. Its boundaries were policed, its entry points were surveilled, but it always existed as a space of freedom outside the pervasiveness of domestication in post-industrial civilization. Let's not forget, I repeat, that the "gay underworld" was hardly just the gays, but precisely that world penetrated by all types of deviants, perverts, whores, pimps, impresarios, night club owners, mafia, gangsters, spooks, intelligence services of all kinds—just see the Dark Ocean Society and you will understand. The Dark Ocean Society of Japan is the key to understanding all modern political and social organization because underneath the pervasiveness of the domestication and management of modern civilization, underneath its superficial orderliness, there remained the "floating world," the free world as a still and dark ocean in which moved monsters, including the lords and crafters of this new civilization themselves. They still live in that world, not in ours. Our world is the house of subjection, they live in the estate of freedom and power. It is only that, with the relatively large number of gays that exist, this world was much larger than it is now, and more varied, its entry points more penetrable. The space of night that gays created for themselves, in which such types could at least *feel* they had new opportunity to expand and act, was nuked in the 1980's with AIDS first of all, and then at the same time with the "gay rights" and "gay identity" movement, through which they came "into the open," and became the worst and most merciless enforcers of the global slave state. But enough about them: you must understand! I use this as illustrative and true example of what happens to *all* higher types in our time. The vast majority don't

69

become gay, but the plight of the gay is the most simple and therefore instructive example of this. Anyone born with a will to conquest and expansion, any specimen born to courage and the expansion of boundaries, will feel thwarted now, will awaken at a young age to find themselves in a world pervaded by an evil and smothering shadow that seeks to blot out their spirit and break them. How one *responds* to this...that is different. And the responses are various. Look at litter of pups, of whatever species, some will be inquisitive, playful, seek to experiment, to push boundaries, to leave gaze of parents and the old, to conquer space; others will be far more docile and will lack curiosity. The only ones who survive the modern education "whole," not to speak of the regime of modern medication, are precisely those in the litter who are born docile. And more to the point; who can look at the beaten-down males of today and think that a boy who inside him has the spark of conquering spirit won't have anything but disgust for their clownish parody of masculinity! What matters here is which way the spirit turns, and if it can survive the obstacle course of domestication that modern life and the modern education imposes on the best. "Homosexuality" in our age, in any case, is unlike any behavior in the past: as a total phenomenon, it represents one of the characteristic ways that some of the most unusual specimens respond to domestication and are broken by it. Modern homosexuality is a form of vacuum behavior and stereotypy.

34

As sad as the story of many of the modern gays is, the story of the modern transsexual is the same in all ways, but worse. This explains also why so many traps are obsessed with Hegel. They *know in their blood*—but they misunderstand themselves and forget who broke them. The story of the modern transsexual is the story of our collective future.

35

Should the tyranny that has descended on our age ever gain the power it seeks and then be challenged enough to feel itself in danger, the mass annihilations that will be carried out by homosexual, transsexual, and especially lesbian commissars will exceed in scale and cruelty anything that has yet happened in known history. Imagine lesbian mulatta commissars with young Martin Sheen face and haircut manning the future Bergen-Belsens, installations that will span tens of miles.

36

Barbarism and Civilization—It's funny when Westerners defer to China or the old cities of the Near East and the Orient as the fountains of civilization, the standards of city life: "we're latecomers, we were in loincloths in forest with painted face hunting boar while they had cities and writing." This true, but Westerner forgets what civilization means. Less myopic than others, but still myopic, he thinks when he hears Chinamen lived in cities for five thousand years, that these must be like the cities in his own history. There are cities and cities. But what was writing? Most of it was for inventory or the most tedious kind of national or dynastic chronicles. Lists and lists: the kinds of passages that make the young bored even with the Bible. The oldest part of Greek literature is from the *Iliad,* the catalogue of ships: the heroes and their retinues are recounted with much flourish and poetry, so it's not so boring, but is just barely saved by Homer's artistry. But nearly every national "writing" is like this, and most "writing" stayed in that condition for a long time. Chinese have always lived in houses, yes, if that's all you mean by "civilization"; but their history is marked by convulsions of annihilation. Just look in their history, the Cultural Revolution is the norm: mass extinction of millions of faceless peasants in the name of remaking a new society. They are no hive: they ignore the dead in the street and look away. I've known of ravens who have more consideration for one of their own. Everything for oneself, everything for personal utility: a pleasure in cruelty toward the weak and toward animals. This is the end-result of thousands of years of "civilization." Don't be fooled by the supposed historical self-conception of such people. Many periods of forgetfulness, when they erased and threw away their chronicles even and totally falsified their history (small example even today: they teach that Genghis Khan was a Chinese general...) This true for many other civilizations. Even religious texts: leaving aside the problem of translation, the Koran is, as Schopenhauer claimed, a tedious book of wretched, repetitive stupidity, with not a single new idea in it, "the poorest form of theism." Unfortunately this is sufficient for the level of most people's religious needs. Is not clear that writing is a great advance, for much of history…its value is questionable. Only quite late some productions of genius arise that redeem the skill of writing. In similar way, different societies mean quite different things by "city." In the Orient this has always referred to a steaming pile of humanity, with crowded, fetid eateries, close-packed throngs wading through shit and the filth of animals, rabbit and hen kept in cages, abused orphans, endless drone of yelling humangs hawking wares and spitting phlegm on street. You see this still in the cities of the Far East. Even in Japan, that all love for its supposed order, there is a terrible menace hanging on the streets of Tokyo that drives too many of the good people there to the mental asylum. The workplace is hell and transportation system is chaotic and suffocating, it reduces everyone again to the cipher he has always been in the Oriental city... a shadow even in his home where the woman inhabits all the terror of the ancient family deities. The Japanese man gets allowance from wife, who often physically depletes him, takes his phone allowance, his lunch money. The woman rules Vietnam, and the faceless clerk or merchant who claws his path in the antheap of this society is beholden to his hectoring wife like slave. Matriarchy and anonymity are the principles of these piles of biomass—never call them hives! The hive is noble: the hive can be a work of beauty and order, but the city, the city in its original form, is humanity reduced to a steaming ratpile. In the hive the ant or bee achieves the full development of its inborn nature as worker or warrior or queen, but who can say this of most cities in history—do you think man stamping papers, scheming to escape wrath of long-nailed office autocrat with spittoon, who hawks smoked fish out of newspapers with fingerless gloves or sells birds with clipped wings to jeering hueman macacas, do you think such creature is a specimen of well-turned out life? And the more depressing possibility that, for the vast majority, such life *is* the expression, the full expression of their inborn reach and wants, still it must be the case that they were selectively bred by their masters to this degraded and zombified form. But even the scared and huddled ash-and-sallow-faced schemer of Saigon or Chengdu was in his remote ancestry like the free Black Yi who terrorized the Han as recently as a hundred years ago, or the powerful-bodied, self-sufficient Tibetans who have made sport of them for centuries. Existence for such life is hell, trapped not only in a miserable society of anonymity, but in a body bred for such a society. Still there must be a spark they can never extinguish, that at least asks for *all this to stop.* Do you understand what Buddhism is now? No, look north: to the Manchus and other Tungus-peoples hardened in the taiga and the Arctic, to the freedom-loving Mongols who to this day love nothing more than to drive out into open country with no roads and consider our cities horribly claustrophobic. Actually in history when you look at life of true nomads who are always on the move and in open space, they never engage in the kind of depressive introspection and questioning of life that you only see in settled and civilized peoples. The Buddha became a world-denier in the city—look at his conversion, what drove him to it! It is the injustice but above all the *filth,* the disgusting suffocation of city life, the vision of life degraded and under distress, that led him to his *escape*...he said, "the home is a place of filth." And what was this escape, after all, but just an attempt to re-establish the freedom and openness of the steppe, where man can once again be what he was born to be? He thought he was opening up a steppe of the spirit, and in the *sangha,* the brotherhood of disciples and monks, he was re-creating that true secret society of the steppe, the society natural to a man like him, the brotherhood of warriors and the free youths! In such way you must also understand "the West," or actually the city of the West. The small, orderly city of the north Italians, the German and Swiss cities Machiavelli praises for how well-run they are, this is entirely alien to the Orient, and indeed to all other civilized societies that we know of. The very idea of the citizen is alien to civilization as such. In the respect for privacy, for distance, for property and propriety—in the *small* and orderly character of the cities, in the relentless concern of the aristocracy with biological quality, you see an attempt to *mitigate* the great evils of civilization. Actually you see an attempt to reestablish some of the character of barbaric and free life inside the city, if only for the citizen class, or the upper class. If there can be any defense of civilization it is this, that historically it gave a class the full or nearly full benefits of the free life of the steppe and forest and mountain while ridding them of some of its inconveniences—at the price, of course, of misery for the vast majority. In nearly all other parts of the world but the West, the misery inside civilization was universal and the elite, such as it was, didn't redeem this misery: they themselves remained servile. A city means nothing, but could even mean a retrogression in the human type. If the only civilizations that had existed were all like Han China, then the choice between barbarism and civilization would be easily made in favor of barbarism, of free Mongol life.

37

The modern city is a monstrosity, but it doesn't yet approach the anonymous squalor of Oriental civilization, of *default civilization.* It's a contradictory place but you see a counter-drive even in the attempt to preserve *parks*. This exists in Tokyo, in many European and European-derived cities like Buenos Aires—its makers must have been obsessed with preserving some piece of nature inside the city, and hired the French to beautify it—and in non-Western cities that have copied this way. In the arrangement of public spaces as well, of the streets, and even of the social life, the modern city is not entirely a reversion to the pre-modern squalor of pure civilization, but an attempt to preserve or at least simulate a natural space for man to move, to expand, to practice and perfect some excellences, as limited or stunted as these may be. In the modern world the return of pure civilization is the slum and the shantytown. It is slowly but certainly encroaching on the modern city as it still exists, which is in all ways a left-over from European domination of the world, and is by no means the form toward which life is progressing. The future of *Blade Runner* is much too optimistic, and even that in *Elysium* doesn't approach the true wickedness of our fate if nothing is done. Mohammed Atta, one of the leaders of the 9/11 plot, was an architecture student. He was deeply moved by what had happened to Aleppo, and the corruption of Muslim life that finds itself disoriented in the modern city, not just in its different moral life, but in the arrangement of space and buildings that upsets the life of the faithful. He was reacting to the modern city as such, not necessarily to the slum, although the expansion of modern life in the third world is very ambiguous here; there's always some slumification. The cities of the Near East, of North Africa, of most of the Muslim world and even much of the Orient, were in any case always differently arranged from the West, having neighborhoods closed off physically from each other, walled compounds with inner courtyards, and in general a turning away from public, political space, into the space of the family and the clan. This was a result not only of the corruption of authorities, but of an entirely different feeling of what the city existed for in the first place. There is a confusion about what different peoples object to in the modern world: they don't necessarily hate in the modern the same thing you hate in it. I would rather ally with the leftist hipster than with China! The Chinese will actually "appropriate" everything and pretend they invented it.

38

Aristotle says Greeks are different from north Europeans and the Orientals. The Asian is civilized but slavish; the European barbarian is uncivilized, unlearned, but free. In this formula is assumed Aristotle believed in a "balance" between these two extremes, and that Greeks were better because they were the "median" between these two deficient extremes. Actually neither Aristotle's view nor the view of the Greeks of his time, and even later, took things quite this way. There was no equivalence drawn between the free northern barbarian and the slavish Asian, but the Greeks valued and respected the free barbarian far more than the Asian. You can see this is so from many things: as late as the Crusades, when Anna Comnena wrote the *Alexiad*, she refers with some horror but also much respect to the Western barbarians. She is in awe at their handsomeness, their bravery and often their intelligence and cunning. Similar praise never exists for the civilized or slavish peoples of the Near East. The same attitude existed also in the age of the classical Greeks. Herodotus among others expresses much admiration for the Scythians and sees them as the innovators of a new and magnificent way of life, the nomadic, through which they confounded and defeated Darius and the Persians. Very often you can read of classical Greeks who, perched on the shores of the Black Sea, "went native" at least for part of the year and joined the nation of the Scythians, in admiration of their free life. The same thing happened much less often, and usually not at all, in the Near East: there were mercenaries, artisans, architects that worked for the Persian king and others, but they didn't go native in this way (the charge, "to Medize," referred to a political alignment taken out of necessity, not to a cultural preference or affinity for a way of life). The Athenians used Scythians as police in their city, but, aside from a few very old families with claims to Phoenician heritage, there was no equivalent use of Orientals and Asians, except as slaves. The beauty of northern European children is praised in antiquity very late: children of Angles for sale are referred to as "not Angles, but angels." Many of the Greek heroes and gods had fair hair and blue or grey eyes, among which, Aphrodite, Athena, Apollo, Achilles, Menelaus, and many others; many ancient poets refer to the Dorians as a blond race. It's hard to believe that such idealization would have been made for the qualities of neighboring nations that were despised. No, from all this and more it's clear the Greeks admired the power and freedom of the barbarian far more than the "civilized" way of the slave, and his false intelligence. And the "balance" often attributed to Aristotle between these two ways is no such thing, but a reference to what I speak of here, that Western civilization, the European city, is unusual because it is the attempt to preserve free and barbaric life within the confines of the city. It's an attempt to exalt and develop certain tendencies of that free life that could presumably benefit from the arts, the science, and the leisure that can only be promoted inside a city. It's an exception in history. And by settled city and settled life, I mean settled with SLAVES! And let's not forget that the Greeks never abandoned that mobile and nomadic life, but transposed it to the sea, as to a large extent the Germanic peoples also always have—they've always been a seafaring people. Entire Greek cities, like those of the Phocaeans, rather than submit to Persian rule preferred to embark their ships and move to colonies as far away as France and Spain—Marseille was founded by them, but there were outposts farther west as well. The Athenians were ready to do the same to escape subjection, and like the Scythians, take to the open sea in their sea-wagons, which in fact they did for a while. The call of the open steppe, the freedom of the new steppe of the seas, this never left them. It's clear from this and even more how much contempt they had for the civilized and slavish life of the Asian, and how much respect and longing they had for the life of the free barbarian. This extended in some way even to their respect for the blaq Ethiopian, about who Herodotus says such nice things, especially when he compares them to the neighboring Egyptians. But in this case, there was very little familiarity with the African, his nature too foreign to the Greek, and there was the suspicion, supported by Aristotle and many others, that the African and also the Arab were too stupid to represent an admirable alternative. Nevertheless in spirit I would say even now the European has much more in common with the African than with the "Asian," meaning the inhabitant of the broad swathe of land stretching from Han China to the Near East, that includes the long-settled farming *serf* regions of the planet. I know many dorks who fetishize IQ above all else will disagree with this. The Orient and Asia has always been the enemy...Africa is mostly irrelevant. The "African" may even be an ally and only became a problem under conditions of modern mass democracy, when he has been manipulated and stirred up by others.

39

Some of the modern right wing is "environmentalist," and even beyond this, but mostly has contempt for the left Greens and other half-and-half because they misunderstand the problem of civilization and of technology. The problem of modern left is they seek not to defend nature, but to blame the West for the modern condition. And this is because the problem is said to be technological or "civilizational" progress as such. These people don't understand that the rapacious life, the buglife, is the default condition of mankind and that the West along with a couple of others has attempted, since its beginnings, to try mitigate the evils of "pure civilization" and to bring the benefits of free life within civilization, as far as this was possible. The left environmentalist is not a reliable defender of nature: he's "anti-racist" first and cares for nature second. Actually the two things are incompatible. China and India are by far the sources of the most serious *obvious* pollution, which is the destruction of the world's oceans with plastics and garbage. The contempt for animal life is rare in India—Schopenhauer says it's for this reason that they easily rejected Christianity, because they heard of the gross mistreatment of animals in Europe of the time—but animal cruelty and abuse is exceedingly common and the rule in China and most of the rest of the non-European world. It is only Indian and, today, European man that is moved by compassion for animals, who are our brothers and sisters. The practice of industrial agriculture is a great evil that must be stopped, but who besides European man really cares for this? Others seem to take a great joy in the humiliation and torture of even cats and dogs. Furthermore it is, as is well known, the zombi hordes of the third world that care nothing for public and national parks and that are the ones who litter and exploit them, often by flinging feces as they've long learned, being sons of the honey badger that eats its own shit. As is well known, the Sierra Club and other environmentalist organizations used to oppose mass immigration, in part quietly for this reason, but also because population increase will on its own place unacceptable strains on nature. The populations of Europe and Japan, under the strain of life in high population density in the late 20th Century, chose to limit their fertility, and there's nothing wrong with this: it is the governments, corrupt and under the lash of financiers dependent on population increase, that forbad a natural retrenchment of population. Therefore the modern left, "anti-racist," pro-migrant, can never really be environmentalist. But, even more, in the promotion of the third world "primitive" (he is no such thing) and the false belief that life there is easier on the environment, they promote the slum, the shantytown, "civilization," the locust default existence of mankind. It's true that the non-Western man lives "closer to nature" in terms of his material needs, but this doesn't translate into a more natural life or less stress on resources: he uses any excess to breed indiscriminately and make more like himself. Any aid to Africa or much of the rest of the third world doesn't translate into improved quality of life, even into improved nutrition, but is immediately converted into more children who continue to live at the same level of misery. The true environmentalism is racism and has a racial foundation, and in fact the two things, environmentalism and racism, are indistinguishable. This is why there's endless discussion of "global climate change," because it takes attention away from concrete problems that are within our grasp to solve—the destruction of national parks, of public spaces, of the mistreatment of animals, and most especially of the oceans. All of these problems are problems of race, not of the modern city as such, modern progress, or the progress of technology. In fact, the attempt to limit this progress and to screw back humanity or freeze it in some supposedly pre-modern form, the attempt for example to bring back "small communities" in the modern world, is the greatest danger and a possible source of the most thorough-going and totalitarian subjection.

40

The true understanding of peasants you aren't going to get from those modern windbags who extol their life or that of "noble savage"; but more likely to get from Chekhov's story of that name. They are a wretched bunch, and locusts on the earth. You can get a good image of them also from Kurosawa movie like *Seven Samurai.* The peasant and serf, the default state of mankind has, like animal, his nose directed toward the earth and the ground, because it is there that the objects of *interest* are found, the needs of bare life. He is far from contemplation even of the stars, that Homer says gladden the heart of the shepherd alone on mountain. The dwellers of the valleys and tillers of the soil are the prototype for all the modern "bugmen," don't be fooled otherwise. *This* is the "frame" or worldview that turns all matter and all things into mere utilities. It doesn't need technology to do so, and never has. In primitive farming societies they will immediately execute any of the intelligent as a witch: this is still done in Africa and there is the famous Chinese saying about how the intelligent must be killed. This is always the case in much so-called "primitive" life, life under the thumb of the empowered old matriarchs and the conceptual dildoes they use to clobber the heads of young men. What is worst about the modern world is the reimposition of this life, which is taking place for political and biological reasons. The problem of our time has never been with technology as such. There is no inner working of technology that inevitably leads to human subjection. The tendency exists merely because, by allowing an overwhelming increase in the numbers of the superfluous, it gives them and those who cater to them power when it is mixed with democracy. The left environmentalist, among many others, is misguided because he wants *more* power given to such people. He attacks precisely those elements of the modern West, of modern technology, even of modern culture, that can mitigate somewhat the rule of the superfluous and their destruction of nature, including human nature. I can imagine few fates worse than if we decided to "live closer to our means," to retrench and stop technological progress and innovation, to scale back to "small, integral communities," to bring back "traditional forms" in our circumstance. I understand the desires of those on the right who long for the great parts of the past, but understand this: any such attempt *in the modern world*, I mean to promote the small village, the rustic life, the modest life, will lead not to the reestablishment of the glories of past ages, but to the freezing of modern corruption, to its stabilization and permanence. You will get small communities run by the gynocracy, to suppress true manhood and youth, but this time with the benefit of whatever modern technology is already around. They will do so in the name of "traditional virtue." They will be Christian, maybe, but their Christianity will be a cover for Marxism in one way or another. It doesn't matter what ideology or religion or "ideals" you give them, they will still behave the way they're born to. The problem of the modern world, as also of the degradation of the environment, isn't technology or a way of life or an ideology, but the ubiquity and rule of *a certain kind of human....* and until this problem is solved..........

41

I don't know if the wardens of this prison and owners of this space are present or not, but I suspect they are. I don't think we live just in some impersonal emergent mechanism, a "system" that entraps everyone, something like "managerialism," or "post-industrial *ennui*." I think all of this was consciously crafted. It's possible much of known history is falsified. Nietzsche among many others hinted at this. I don't think we can ever know who these individuals are, but I suspect they walk among us like average men. I once knew a woman of Rockefeller branch—and let me say, this is exactly what I *don't* mean by these hidden powers I'm talking about, you don't know their names—but she went to vegetable shops or on subway without anyone knowing who she was, without jewelry, and had only contempt for the known rich who have to walk with retinues and bodyguards and are under constant surveillance by media and others. What could they want, then, you ask, if not to enjoy and show wealth? Just that, freedom and power, that everyone else lacks. They live outside all law and constraint, we are but the material and fodder for their hunger. Their schemes are demented: the movie *Mulholland Drive* revealed some of what they do, indirectly and with metaphor. They have learned how to harness various kinds of energy, for example, the kind of energy bestowed by human attention in large numbers, and to power certain kinds of machines with it. The attention that Hollywood gets is received and absorbed by a machine of great power, that amplifies it and serves some use. They founded this rite with human sacrifice and human blood, and that is what this movie is about. They know how to harness sexual energy, which is why they persecuted Wilhelm Reich but stole his technology. Trump's family knows the secrets of Tesla. They know many other things: science and rationalism are the "public religion" of our time, but the rulers believe in something quite different. The masses are dazzled by the fridge, the hairdryer, the phone: they live drugged and hypnotized by assurances that the wizards who produce these things are modest engineers who live by publicly known and verified procedures, that they're just quiet men who master unremarkable and docile physical forces. Their comfort is a surety of their faith in the regularity of nature, that has taken divine fear and awe away from them. Meanwhile the world is run by men like Erik Jan Hanussen, or, actually, he was only a tool of others like him, but you don't know their names. Someone wore green gloves in Hong Kong. They live in the realm of power and freedom.

42

Great lie of our age is that it is about the freedom of the senses, liberation of the desires from stodgy social and moral controls. In fact even Middle Ages man lived with more lust for life, even more sexual lust, than the modern: he worked less also. Most of the year there were feast days. There was the minimum amount of work done possible to have enough crops and to pay the taxes, that were relatively small. Most modern men hardly have the property of the medieval freeholder. Hygiene was bad and disease rampant, infant mortality very high: many other problems too. Is not my favorite time. But once you survive childhood, work is the great difficulty in life, it's the curse of Adam: go to small book shop in Thailand, you find complete chaos among the books on sale there. If you ask the owner why he doesn't arrange alphabetically or some other way, he will say, because would be too much work and I make enough as it is. But in this one thing, "Merry Old England," for example was a place of joy and drunkenness and feasts. They drank ale without hops, but used gruit made from heather and other herbs: this drink they had all day, filling them with passion for life...beer at this time was a stimulant and aphrodisiac. They considered the water-drinker much like we look at the dry hipster herb who stirs caffeine-free rooibos and looks at you with dour eyes. It was the Puritans who introduced hops, precisely to make beer bitter and unpleasant, and to turn it from a stimulant into a soporific that kills the sexual instinct in man. But before this, the people of England had surely more intense sex0rz, if that's how you measure things. Actually it's how you should measure things because it's a sign of something else. A life of great and real joy or passion is a life receptive to certain other instincts and desires, that *also* come from nature, but that the modern lords of lies are terrified of. It is *these* others that they want to suppress, at least for the laity. The sexual irritation that the many are kept under is different from the kind of unencumbered and carefree, passionate and demonic lust you found in premodern times, and that you still find in pockets of the Third World. This modern parody of lust drains all energy, that other true lust sets the heart on fire with many other wild enthusiasms: Paglia is wrong, they will never allow her brand of "feminism" to flourish; it would defeat the purpose! Entire purpose of modern education is to suppress that enthusiasm, to make you second-guess yourself when you hear the voice of old friends...goading you on.....And yes, they achieve this by promoting the tedious, exhausted sexual irritation you find among the obese, the "polyamorous," the weirdo old tribesmen who get off on exposing themselves to women. This pervasive irritation blinds the many also to receptivity to these *other* desires I'm talking about. "Telepathy" is public and mythical version of something real. This is same way that many religions teach metempsychosis because truth of reincarnation is too impersonal and too hard to grasp. It's not out of the question that we are constantly receiving motions inside the unity of things from many inanimate objects, some possibly on the other side of the known universe, but occasionally from people we know, trees, and many other objects. We may have close bond on this level with individuals related to us, even in the future, or an intimation of those that the genius of the species intends as our mate, because it wants the production of this or that child at this or that moment. The most significant of these "telepathic" connections is indeed when two such people, supremely suitable for each other on a biological path, *recognize* in each other this inner intention or striving of nature for the production of something—of course they think it's about something very different. In the normal case this is almost always man and woman, for production of a certain child, that nature wants to bring into emergence. But on rare cases there can be other reasons for similar connection in will, such as, two friends who are intended to achieve some task together. "We reach out with open arms in anticipation of satisfying our desire or delusion, meanwhile nature achieves her secret intention": it is so in the birth of certain children, but also of other things. The suspicion of friendship that the "ghey rights movement" promotes has worked to destroy this. Women are likely to be able to receive such messages more than others, because in them the intellect is more firmly planted in the body and the inborn will. Many times this means they are, more than others, slaves of utility, but it also means they live more in the moment, less encumbered by concepts and abstractions, have more access to direct perception of things. They can see through many lies and can know people's intentions before they know what they want themselves. Saddam Hussein was like this: he was a transsexual in his soul. Not all women, but there are cases where a certain turn in spirit frees their intellect from the confusions of their drives and the chaos of their hormones, and yet they don't lose that rootedness in nature that is usually harder for men to achieve. This is why the Greeks and many other ancient peoples knew that women are more likely to be Oracles and to know the future and also the intentions of others (they "know" the future from innate sensation of the intentions and the blood of others). Cassandra was such a prophetess, and even the great seer Tiresias was said to have turned into a woman for a while. Many shamans practice transvestism among various peoples—fools interpret this as "gay rights," not seeing the cultic understanding of femininity. The Pythia was a woman, and the ancient Germans always consulted women before great decisions, because they could provide a different and more direct view of things. The modern lords of lies have alienated women from this by promoting the hyper-conscious, talky, neurotic-obsessive persona among urban slave women. That is a parody of the worst kind of men. Oracles in nature are already rare enough, and how many have been lost to us because they were misled by the snakes who seduced her into thinking she should ape the snappy, chatty self-consciousness of the midget homosexual and "comedian"? They know how powerless we are without knowledge of the future; they keep this for themselves.

43

Many times in a new country I got so restless in small apartment and filled with such a desire to act out that, if bars and everything else is closed, I go to the nearest hostel and make a nuisance of myself. I was kicked out of a number of such places, and also out of frathouses in the past, when I told them my theories about mind control, about the numbers in phone books arranged in suggestive ways, about the habits of African hunting dogs and the strength of hyena's bite and neck. The people liked my stories, but the staff watched me from the side with great jealousy and wanted to "call security." In mall I've been frequently asked by sallow guard if "Sir, do we have to call security," because, while walking, I felt myself grabbed with a fast *spirit,* and ejaculated all kinds of words in Tourette way. I went to troll gay bars with Hitler mustache, and outraged the patrons there with stories of how the National Socialists started out as a gay-rights movement in a basement in Munich, and how this is admirable. Hunger for space, claustrophobia—the most noble phobia—isn't "just spiritual." Nothing serious is ever just "of the spirit." Of the spirit means fake and gay—all real orientations exist only in the blood and show themselves, not just in the higher reaches and tastes of one's spirit, but in daily life and daily needs. I want always to be in center of room in front of big window when I must work, which I hate doing. All real thoughts come only when you walk outside, standing up, in fresh air: I knew this long before I was made aware of it through Nietzsche, who says you should distrust any thoughts you've had indoors. Add to that, any thoughts that come into your head in the fetid miasma of most cities. Add to that, when the whole day you're harassed and needled by the viciousness of others, that comes from a vulgar desire for power displayed by secretaries, service workers. Service workers have often tried to oppress me. Larry David understands this problem; but he is still trying to be too "nice," he presents his struggle against the oppression of the service industry as self-deprecating, self-criticism. They are mostly vicious demons. Just today waitress came to try to take away coffee cup, even though it had small layer on bottom, my favorite cold layer of coffee....I told her, no I drink this, I signaled with my hand, and still she bend over, while looking me in the eye, trying to take, and I could see in the look in her eye a mixture of defiance, lust, masochistic lust, a desire to usurp, a desire to eat me alive. I had to repeat three times. I've had to push customer service bitchmale against the wall, he wouldn't stop following me around and commenting on the wine. I don't pretend to be a rebirth of Theseus or Ajax, but if any such man were born today, he'd be fast in a mental asylum or dead. Only the small in spirit can thrive. In this way they chip away at your spirit in a thousand ways. Traffic lights train you to obedience like animal in cage, especially at night when there are no other cars around. Having to be in passenger seat while moron is driving, I couldn't even stand this friend and asked him if he wouldn't mind if I jacked off while we drove between two cities. "Yeah man, sure, go ahead no big deal..." he agree, so I know there was nothing left in him. It's for this reason also that I go in the dirtiest of red light districts or enter porn cinemas: I like to see trap injecting industrial-grade silicon in chest, I like to hear whores trade stories how the word "homosexual" comes from "a sexual man," and that homos are just hypersexualized whore-males. I believe this is true.

44

There was night club on top of strange cinema that during the day doubled as place of porn. I decided to go inside once with friend, and old man farther on same row contrived so that he got out right in front of us and brushed right by me, grabbing my crotch. I shoved his face into the wall, and had to push my way past security-guard with terrible breath and goblin-like pockmarked face. There was loose vampire bat in lobby that had flown in, but this normal. Outside on the street as I ran looking for taxi there was black woman taking shit in middle of road. At intersection in gray beaten up Volvo there was a driver with no head and on seeing this I entered a state of vertigo and fugue. Some talk about this "madness behind things." The *real world* is very different from the one that appears to us in waking life, but it's not so different as to be entirely alien or abstract or "philosophical" in the way you might think. It's not abstract, or made of perfect and eternal forms, it's not somewhere else: it's immanent, here, and within things, and it's twisted. It doesn't have any moral significance that can be understood by us. When Heraclitus speaks of all things being one, and all things being *fire,* he means this: when this actually shows itself to you, there is a demoniac and violent madness underlying things. The real world is similar to the apparent, but uncanny, devilish, disordered *for us.* Its hidden order, *the fatal X behind things,* reaches for things and aims beyond our scope as humans: it's why Lovecraft knew it was true, our world is fashioned by a demiurge who is a blind, retarded schizophrenic. Its origin and happenings and its fate is in the play and war of the most gruesome factions, forgotten gods…to them we're like stowaway rats on a ship. This shows itself most vividly in some dreams, which, if they had continuity, we couldn't distinguish from waking life. *Some* but not all of the insane are able to see parts of this world, but they're all unheard prophets, and ever more so in our time…psychiatry, a fraud, has weakened all faith in them, and of them in themselves. Everywhere the signal is jammed.

45

I've always been attracted to the dirtiest and filthiest of the Gnostic sects: the Carpocratians, and later their analogues the Khlysty in Russia, Rasputin's evil coven. They formed groups of women around a great teacher and sorcerer who could drive them into orgiastic madness: the rebirth of the Maenads! Man who plays the wrong way with this ends up being *eaten alive* like Euripides' Pentheus (otherwise an inadequate piece). The Jews had a parallel version, the Frankists. All of these believed that inside us is a spark of divinity that is trapped in matter. Since matter and this world are the work of an evil Demiurge, the laws governing matter and human life as they appear especially in the Bible are the laws of Satan. Therefore to free yourself you must overturn every single one of these laws, you must engage in every act of evil, every crime, every atrocity: only in this way does the gate open out of the kingdom of shadows... only this way you find Paradise and get past the angels guarding its paths. I don't recommend this way! Some say much of the left is motivated by such a faith, its secularized variety. There are, in the case at least of Frankism some weird historical peculiarities: many of the prominent leftist Jews, the founders of the most aggressive leftism at least, are said by some orthodox Jews to be of Frankist origin. This was so in the case of Brandeis; hardly the worst, but supposedly there are many others. I myself don't believe this, though it should be studied. I feel a kinship to such sects, but this not direct: I must explain. In general you can understand Gnosticism, in all its forms, in this way: the Hebrew faith is based in claim "saw that it was good" ...the claim that the world is crafted by a benevolent God and that matter and the world is good. There are only a few other faiths like this: Islam is another, and Schopenhauer claims Greek and Roman paganism are same, although this is not the full truth. Greek optimism is of an entirely different sort than Biblical optimism anyway. But Hinduism and Buddhism see the world as something you must escape, they believe in *nirvana* or *moksa* that frees you from the cycle of rebirths. This is more normal, and a lot more widespread in history. And this is in a sense true since suffering so obviously outweighs its opposite: in any individual life this is true, where moments of happiness are rare and pass quickly. But also, if you imagine the pleasure of an animal eating versus the pain and agony of the animal being eaten, you can't be fooled ...you see that suffering exceeds pleasure or happiness in this world, by many magnitudes. Many bears, some African hunting dogs and others, they bite out of animal before it is even dead. Best, like I said, to be killed by jaguar that dispatches you with quick bite to the skull! Its jaws are strong, grown to bite through turtle. I believe it's the most compassionate cat, but most murder in nature isn't like this. Houellebecq talks about how as a boy he couldn't stand the self-satisfied, dronelike and calm "reasonable" voice of narrators on nature shows, that try to obscure the worst agonies of animals, murder in blood. According to any rational calculation, life is not worth living, because pain far outweighs pleasure. Heavily medicated nihilists are likely to deny this—the blessed and happy know it's true...but also know that reason and rationality are false. Gnosticism is driven by the problem of suffering, or compassion for those who suffer, and tries to absolve God of responsibility for this state of things. Sometimes it says the God of the Bible was put to sleep, or imprisoned himself, or that he is bound with chains of adamantine and kept in a cage, and that a usurper took his place. Other times it says that the God described in Genesis isn't the real God, but a demiurge, and the real God sent his emissary Jesus to overturn the rule of this demiurge. There are many variations, and some interject not one demiurge, but ninety-nine, all to remove responsibility from the Godhead for the creation of this world of evil. They should have just become Buddhist or Hindu and stopped trying to save the mythology of Canaan! Maybe in its beginnings the Christian faith was the same as the Buddhist, and this is now lost in the confusions of hateful sects that distort history. It's easy to think that this is the religion of a hopeless age, that it's a byproduct of the decay of the Roman Empire and the symptom of despair or suffering. It's much worse than that! The problem for man as for other animal isn't stress or suffering, but the feeling that one can't escape: the despair and panic of exhaustion and entrapment. Beyond the borders of the known inhabited world, the *oikoumene*, there lay uncrossable oceans, including the great earth ocean of the steppe, and the Sahara in the other direction. China and India were known, and trade existed, but this was only a vague knowledge that could have, in theory, stimulated the sense of conquest and adventure. There were, in other words, plenty of *possible* sources for the feeling that beyond the known world still remained the unexplored. The same unknown that called the enterprise and spirit of the Portuguese, Spanish and other Europeans who set out on a colonial mission of world-conquest and discovery, all of this existed in late Roman times. But the will or spirit was not there, there was only exhaustion on all sides, the same exhaustion that explains the pointless history of China, India, and all long-settled farming places. Civil wars and palace coups will always continue, but the spirit of man is broken by habituation to an overlong domestication, and nothing genuinely great in body or spirit takes places again after a while. This "habituation" includes of course those "habits of the blood," which leads to the breeding and overproduction of the superfluous. Once a great power imposes domestication on its neighbors and then itself, comforts grow, and so many are born who experience life already at birth in an exhausted state, and who call upon themselves the governments and religions of the exhausted and stressed. Surely the external obstacles we face now are far greater: outer space for us is not traversable even in theory, and we know of nothing on the other side of empty space...everything outside the already known seems barren. And yet, I repeat, this kind of physical limitation isn't the real cause of a spiritual exhaustion that yearns for *escape* of some sort. It is the very character of domestic life to present the world as an enclosed *owned space,* and, although mankind adapts itself on the whole to this condition, both biologically and culturally, yet there remains a glimmer of the opposite tendency inside even the lowliest. He can't help but experience this new state of things in late civilizations except with *dread,* the dread suspicion...an uncanny *suspicion*..... that the world is artificial. He begins to sense that this hothouse he lives in is the malevolent creation of a demiurge that likes to observe our sufferings, that He and his minions feed on them. In the remote future, should the evil of human innovation continue unchecked, we really will live in the world the Gnostics feared, and that spark of vital life and energy that is the gift of nature to all youthful peoples born from its womb, that spark will remain entrapped in "matter wrongly configured," matter entirely foreign to its inborn desires and workings, but fashioned instead for the benefit of something else. In many ways the world we inhabit now already anticipates this living hell of the Gnostics, and the response of those in whom the pain of civilization and modernity is most *advanced,* the transsexuals, unwittingly help to further uncouple reality from nature, and to make our progressive domestication more totalitarian and aggressive. And yet, for yourselves, who wish to fight the encroaching tyranny, remember that in conditions of crisis the "Carpocratian" option, the attraction precisely to the criminal and deviant, can be very great ...but...one here is at the edge of the abyss. And the way you interpret the call of this instinct...

46

I am interested in the falsification of history and possibly of geography. I think mankind is exceedingly stupid and wicked, you can't trust a word you receive. I have no doubt your religions are true, but can you be sure some vicious faction didn't insert itself into the hierarchy of priests some time ago, or of religious authorities, or of *book printers,* and insert all kinds of things that weren't there to begin with? For example, all Old Slavonic copies of the Bible in Russia used to have heavy Gnostic interpolations. This explains the multitude of such sects that sprung up there, including those who castrated themselves, and others like the

Duhobors who make a mockery of the higher and noble nudity by practicing the nudity of the deformed. In the West there were similar things: how do you think the Cathars found such currency in north Italy, in the Rhineland? It wasn't just a new teaching, but very *old* practices and old formulas that found a ready home among a population long prepared to receive them. Some were pre-Christian, while others had spread along with the early Church, and preserved elements of early Christianity mixed in with Manicheanism and Magianism and other even stranger things. Why do you assume then that the main religions that survived are not in fact forgeries? Islam could very well be such a forgery: the Koran is a mishmash of nonsense, and possibly was originally a Syriac Christian devotional book that was re-edited much later. Mohammed was their name for Christ, and the faith originally was a version of Nestorianism that was spread by the Persian king, not by Arabs. The entire history of Heraclius' crusade against Persia, as of Persia's downfall in "battles" against Arabs may be entirely fabricated by both sides, though of course now this lie has long been forgotten. What historical or archaeological evidence is there at all for the existence of a Mohammed? But do you have any idea how speculative the conclusions drawn from archaeology are in general? Just read, for example, the kind of "evidence" they used to establish horse-riding on the great steppe before 1000 BC—a few, maybe not even five or six, bones that *seemed* to look like bits. Life is short; rebirth as a man is uncertain, and may happen a billion years from now: to these pitiful liars to trust your only life? Look at Thucydides, who is a great man and a genius of the ages: he seeks to outdo Herodotus, and this pattern is followed throughout all antiquity. Each great historian was setting out to outdo his predecessor as a rival. Do you think they made some things up? How much do you think then that the scholar, the scribe, the vain "monk"—the "nerd" as a type—is likely to lie? They will lie far more than you think...the nerd more than a Thucydides is possessed by infinitely greater mendacity and also vanity, jealousy, spite and pettiness. Don't you think such people, who, for the longest time in the form of the monk were the *only* keepers and copiers of texts from antiquity, don't you think they would be willing to change the text, to add, and even to make up entire books and authors? Corroborations from "third sources" would be relatively easy to manufacture as well. But anyway, Josephus uses this rivalry among the Greek writers to cast doubt on Greek histories in general, and in this he's not entirely unreasonable. Of course where he's wrong is in supposing that the centrally-controlled archives of the other peoples, like the Egyptians, the Babylonians, or his own, are any more reliable. Nietzsche refers to the falsification of the history of Israel that occurred at some time before Josephus—and I think he was referring to the Maccabees. There is no external record anyway of the Jews existing before the kingdom of the Maccabees—Herodotus never mentions them. But there is evidence that the falsification Nietzsche was referring to is even of a later date. Much of antiquity could have been invented by sects or orders of Christians or even Jews, to make it look like their contrived and artificial, *utilitarian* religions had some basis in human nature or were anticipated by wise men in the past. When, in fact, the entirety of their energy was directed toward suppressing the natural spirit of man, the innate reverence of man for the magnificence inside animals and inside things. In the end, nothing can be trusted, that you can't see and feel yourself.

47

We don't know if all of antiquity, or maybe if large portions of it, was entirely made up by medieval monks or by Italian humanists in the Renaissance...or if some eccentric scholar at Constantinople or a monk in Iberia added entire books and passages to Plato or to others. When Nietzsche says that Plato "studied with the Jews" in Egypt...what does he really mean? Could it be, as some have said, that the Jews are actually themselves a recent invention, a sect of the Arabs in Cordoba, and that this group made up parts of Plato or of Aristotle...or so heavily corrupted their works...perhaps working with scattered groups of monks in Europe and with the Vatican later? What *is* the Vatican—and if it didn't exist before, say, the year 1200, how could you be sure...? Machiavelli mentions that St. Gregory wanted to entirely destroy and blot out all pre-Christian culture, and that these bearded men in black robes smashed temples in their hysterical rages, crushed statues, burned books. How do you really know how successful they were, or *when this actually took place?* How do you know that the legacy of the ancient world that Machiavelli claims they preserved only out of necessity—because they shared Latin as the same language—wasn't almost entirely corrupted by their "transcriptions"? Every new form of life among mankind seeks to blot out the memory of its predecessors, to rewrite the history, and maybe does so literally, corrupting the texts themselves. Is there any evidence the desultory and unfortunate "doctors of the early Church" ever even existed? Augustine is almost surely a complete fiction, and there never was any such man—his pidgin "Greek" is nonsense in that area to begin with, and is rather the makeshift Greek of the medieval monk, maybe living somewhere in Burgundy. You don't need to go that far though. I've heard other less strange, but still wild theories: that the New Testament was written by a Jewish woman, as a parody of Greek tragedy. It was an effort to overturn Roman life and power, "Roman privilege," by means of the Passion story—the dead god as an inversion of Greek mystery cult surrounding Dionysos. Does this sound familiar in our own time, when monstrous historical hoaxes…including the so-called and entirely *fake* "Cold War," during which the United States was funding and arming the Soviet Union the whole time? If Nietzsche believed such things, he would have never put them under his own name or said them openly—but, could it be, when he says that Plato is *unGreek,* that he really means precisely this? Was Plato, or at least many of the works of Plato, the invention of a Byzantine polymath, or of a Benedictine? Such speculations are the opposite of comforting, especially in a world where the consolations and certainty of religion are rare. History has somewhat taken the place that religion had, I mean to provide stability to a world that is otherwise lost in complete confusion and chaos and uncertainty. I want this chaos, because what I want to bring thrives in it. The continuity of history, if not its progress, is that last thread that secular, scientific man, unmoored in the universe on this floating rock, the play of titanic and foreign forces…it's the last connection that he had to any sanity. I want a world of psychosis, I want the end of *his* sanity. What if there is no firm ground to what we receive from history, and the continuity we think we have is actually a jumbled and confused mess—that events from antiquity have been confused with events from the Middle Ages, for example? I found the suggestion of Fomenko, that the Crusades and the Trojan War were really the same event, to be so disorienting that I had to act out in a very vehement and stern way that day later. At the lounge, when the bouncer asked me if "I was on drugs" ...and I pushed his forehead away from me in a gesture of majesty and power. I was soundly beaten up by his goons in the alley. The speculations of Anatoly Fomenko, as well as the so-called "phantom-time hypothesis," which claims that three centuries have been wrongly added to our chronology...this is small stuff. It's very small—From these doubts I was led to many others far more horrific. I've lived a wandering life, and at times I was confused by a strange similarity between certain street corners, the smell of this and that building that I supposed were different, the uncanny likeness of two streets that, years later, I can't tell anymore which was which, or if instead I dreamt it. I believe it needs to be investigated, for example, if Mexico City is not in fact the same as Bangkok, and the so-called Baja peninsula not the same as the Malay. The similarity of dishes like *mole* and Thai curries only lends further support to this hypothesis, as does the *kwak'*ing language of the Oaxacans and Chiapans...it's the same as Laotian. I've heard rumors that as you go inland from Port-au-Prince you start to see the lights of Manila, and that the Caribbean islands are no different from the Philippines. Both enjoy the grilled pork, the rice with cheese, delights like spaghettis with ketchup and hot dogs or spam, and, I hear, certain other things also. The slums of Bangkok are the same as those of Mexico City, and Cambodia is the same as Guatemala

(Honduras is entirely fake). Thus it is said in some corners, when Columbus came upon Cuba, it really was Cipangu, or Japan, and he really did discover Asia. The entire New World (and many other areas of the world also) is thus a fraud of the first order. Shanghai can be accessed in two hours from Manhattan by secret bullet train. And if you ask how it is that so many travel by plane, well, it's not so hard for there to be an understanding among the relatively *few* active pilots to keep this a secret and use circuitous routes to make flight-time seem a lot longer. If you don't want to go this far, remember how they can, nevertheless, keep entire continents or islands a secret—you're not allowed, as far as I know, to approach the North or South Poles, and it's not out of the question that a tropical refugium exists in both. There is an esteemed scholar from Bangalore who points out that the year in the Vedas has six months of daylight and six months of darkness.

48

But you think I'm promoting idea of "noble savage"? Do you understand your visions of what is "noble savage" are just a miniature over-spent *China,* a spiritual China on a smaller scale? I know there no such thing as noble savage: Mark Twain attacked the Red Man as a faithless liar and rogue. Well, fine. That doesn't bother *me:* my idea of noble and vital power is different. But...choose whatever view of nobility you will, it doesn't matter, you won't find it among primitives as a rule. You idolize peasants. You look up to island savages living "at one with Nature," I ask you to see what happened to Margaret Mead, and how the

Polynesians punked her—most of the things she wrote about their views on life, about their sexual freedom, was nonsense they made up to make her look foolish. In same way the fools like Gimbutas and others who believe that mankind at some remote point lived under a benevolent matriarchy, again, "at one with Nature," in balance with the needs of the soil and such: sheer nonsense. Everywhere historians, archaeologists find what we thought was matriarchy was really no such thing. You see this in the *Odyssey* where it is clear that the right of succession belongs to he who is husband of Penelope, and Odysseus' son Telemachus isn't assured of his inheritance of the kingdom. Local priestess of the rites of fertility, of the flowering and blooming of the seasons of the earth, who made crops assured to spring from the soil: priestess of the local earth goddess or spirits—whoever married this woman was given a certain prestige or legitimacy as king. This much is true, but it was men who decided who she married, and they decided the sovereignty of the kingdom as well. Everywhere you look to find any kind of formal matriarchy you see that in reality it was nothing of the sort, but something very much like this. When you find polyandry as among some inhabitants of the Himalayas, it is men sharing a woman for lack of resources or because of some other circumstance. By what mechanism could, after all, women rule since they are so much weaker physically, and seem unable to politically organize without men? But...but...there *is* way for them to rule. And so the debunkers of matriarchy are correct but don't see far enough into social relations among primitives, and even the civilized, to realize that matriarchy of a sort is a reality. I already spoke before of one kind. But you find among the Chinese, the Sicilians, that household is run by grandmother. When many of you moderns pine for "communal living," and talk about inter-generational households...you seem to forget that this would mean subjection to a strong-willed Dragon or Gorgon lady. The modern girl, when she pines for the community of the pre-modern extended family imagines that she gets from it the emotional and social support of her female cousins, and a crew of servants in the grandmothers, not the reality...which is utter subjection to the mother-in-law. The modern southeast Asian whose ancestors have lived in Oriental "cities" for generations is completely beholden to his wife...read any anthropological study written before 1970 to see the truth about Asian social life. In Africa, the men are utterly defeated and beholden to matriarchy in complicated ways: the women run all food production without the help of the men, who rely on them for the daily ration of bland sop mushed up from grains. At times to break this monotony they seek bushmeat, but they mostly live as farmers dependent on big-armed woman tending messy patch of roots. The entire social life in this area is managed through secret societies. The apparent political power is brittle and meaningless: interlocking secret societies, based on the manipulation of black and white magic, are the true source of all important decisions reached in the village and even in the cities. Women play a prominent role in such societies, or outright rule them: there is among them a long tradition of respect for woman as *oracle,* which is only natural. The Yoruba water priestess chimping out in ecstasies over the boa, receiving visions, this is not so different from the Pythia. But where the Pythia had submitted to the solar and boyish manliness of Apollo, such a conquest of the power from under the earth never took place in Africa, nor in many other places. And so here as elsewhere there *is* a kind of matriarchy, but it works covertly, so that both the "left" and the "right" are fooled on this point. In the end then the "left" is more correct: the worship of the titanic powers of the earth, of the Great Mother, is connected to a kind of matriarchy, but where they're wrong is in imagining that this leads to any kind of freedom, that it represents a kind of liberation from the strictures of modern civilization, the pain of specialization, the submission to moral authority, the modern "alienation," and every other thing they like to blame. In fact everything that you hate about modern life and that makes it into an Iron Prison—and I agree it is a prison—represents a return of the endless sallow night of matriarchy. It is a *return* in every way, you must understand this literally! Nietzsche says that in the modern Europe you see the reassertion of pre-Aryan modes of life, the return of socialism, of the longhouse, of feminism, and that this is happening also to us internally, where the higher instincts of the spirit are being overtaken physiologically by the retrograde and prehistoric. The life of the village and of the primitive is one of utter subjection, total domestication and total brokenness. The "matriarchy" that does exist, and that exerts enormous influence and power in the social and moral realm, is only the manifestation of this brokenness of the males. Communal solidarity absorbs and snuffs out any personal distinction or intelligence and this task is relatively easy where it concerns the majority of the parts of the village: the real problem becomes what to do with the young males. In every way they represent a threat to the established customs and the physiological torpor that benefits the old and the women. *The* social problem in primitive tribes as well as most civilized and unfree societies becomes this, what to do with the young males, their aggression, their sexual instincts: in every way they must be broken and subsumed for the benefit of the tribe. This is more or less easy for the majority, who lack life force in any significant quantity, harder for the remainder, and where impossible—the fate of the outcast, or, more likely, death. You fool yourself if you imagine that "young males are needed for protection from external threat." In fact most societies of the settled, primitive and as well as civilized, are more than willing to accept the risk of submission to an alien tribe. In a given area, if many such tribes follow this same path of self-domestication the risk is hardly even that great in one's own lifetime and a few benighted, spineless "warrior" drones are sufficient to contend against similar neighbors. But even in cases where there is great external threat from vigorous tribes, such societies, ruled by women, the old, and the imbeciles, are willing to rather accept subjection to the alien than to allow freedom and flourishing for their young men. They are right in this calculation too: subjection to an alien force rarely means extermination at its hands, whereas allowing their own youths freedom and power would end their way of life for good. But submission to the alien just often means some sporadic taxation that used to be relatively hard to enforce: peasants are very good at hiding stores of goods, and even fields. The routine humiliations of subjection, the loss of honor, the rare but occasional rapes, the loss of sovereignty means little to such people. They are allowed to continue their communal life unchanged under the subjection of another, and even thrive under such subjection. They prefer it, anyway. This is the condition of the so-called "old civilizations" of mankind, and especially China and India. The Chinese Han faced the most dreadful external threats from the steppe, and were frequently conquered by a few scattered men on horseback that they outnumbered many times over. They didn't care: their stolid, unchanging life as a community continued, whether it was Jurchen or Mongol or Black Yi that preyed on them. The Indians, once they reached their period of priestly rule and senescence, also degenerated to this condition: they were conquered every summer by adventurers and warlords from the Hindu Kush and beyond. Afghanistan ruled India. But subjection suited them. Slowly, with the patience that yeast enjoys because time is on its side, the Chinese would *wait:* "the day will come when this conqueror too will become exhausted, his blood spent; then he will join us, *the people.*" And they were right. This is the famous assimilation of Chinese civilization, the assimilation of the exhausted and spent. And there's no real way to understand the Chinese other than the reduction of the human animal to mere life: they are not what you understand normally when you say "civilization," but rather a perpetual subject population, a uniform and undifferentiated blob of serfdom that seeks subjection and undermines through it. This is the rule of matriarchy. The Indians and many others are the same. The Chinese on many occasions preferred this path to the alternative, of letting their own men assert themselves and gain the sovereignty. On the brief occasion in the 15th century when they began to have a navy, with its glimmers of freedom and empowerment for youths, they noticed the ferment and disorder that this brought to their society and immediately quashed the whole project. Such societies can't change their condition even if they want to: the interests of *mere life* are too entrenched. The way of settled life is just this then: to break the youths from early age, to take the boys and caponize them physically, mentally and spiritually. This happens in the smallest tribes as well. When they become civilizations, they look much like Han China, or the *sinkhole* cities of the Aztecs, Babylonians, and others. You see here why people like Evola, Jung, Guenon and all their followers go the wrong way. There is only this: whether life is stunted and broken by a "tradition," or whether it is one of the very few, the rare exception, that allows the ascent of life. As a rule, life is stunted and deformed by huemans. This is why huemans are disgusting as an animal, and must be overcome. This is the "free and primitive life" of the noble savage, this is the "matriarchy" that keeps its faith to nature in "sustainable" form. In fact the society of the grass hut is hardly sustainable: such places are rapacious of natural resources, and often vicious to animals and vicious tyrants to people. A good parody of such a society on a small scale is the movie *The Beach.* The rule of weakness is *not* good but something of incredible cruelty, even cannibalism. Cannibalism is the way of all *yeast* life, to which the human animal degenerates under these conditions of gynocracy. Cannibalism is the eternal way of those erased huemans who submit themselves to the Venus Willendorf and all "earth mammies," because this faction of nature is a putrid evil dripping blood from its claws and seeking the dissolution of all higher life, spiritually and biologically, to the amorphous muck of the primeval swamp. If you traveled in Europe around maybe 3000 BC or so you would find wise-eyed cowlike black-haired Neolithic matrons overseeing vast villages of longhouses where lived the hueman animal, fifty or a hundred to a room, with sheep and goats, wallowing in its own shit, tilling the soil, eating those of its members deemed to be "chosen by the gods"—anyone, man or woman, distinguished by vital spirit—and she might even smack you on the head with a lingam-dildo and question your privilege as a traveler. This is the condition of most of mankind until recently, and it is the suffocating miasma to which the modern world is fast *returning,* inside and out.

But enough of this prison. I suppose you want to know of a way out, or, at least, to hear of a different way of life?

Part Three: Men of Power, and the Ascent of Youth

49

Life appears at its peak not in the grass hut village ruled by nutso mammies, but in the military state. In Archaic Greece, in Renaissance Italy and in the vast expanse of the heroic Old Stone Age, at the middle of the Bronze Age of high chariotry, lived men of power and magnificence in great numbers. We are in every way their inferiors. Physically, spiritually and in intellect they exceed us in every way. I give example: our elite athletes, our special forces operators, are nothing compared to them. We find Paleolithic bones, the femur, so robust that nothing from our runners or power-lifters equals. These men were capable of sustained speeds unimaginable today. You know about Marathon, but not the whole story. The real physical feat wasn't just the soldier who ran the twenty miles or so back to Athens to warn the people. The entire army ranged on the beach in heavy bronze armor, facing the enemy. After the Persians landed, the Greeks charged them from more than a mile away. The Persians were amazed at the line of gleaming bronze running toward them and their war cry. These men ran a mile in very heavy armor and also carried six-foot-plus ashen spear-spike. They drove the invaders into the sea. And right after this great effort they marched, still in armor, all the way back to Athens without pause, to prevent the Persians from making an opportune landing there. I don't think any special military units would be able to equal this feat today, and these were the average citizens of Athens.

Still more, they exceeded us the same way in mind and spirit: their sophists were able to remember fifty names, and more, upon hearing them once. Some had the gift of remote vision, that the Rosicrucians pine for, and that the Soviet and American intelligence services have attempted to rediscover in vain. Here we have life at its peak. You know about their great art, science, and literature, or think you do. But these were men of conquest, exploration and adventure *first*. Aeschylus had on his tombstone engraved that he fought at Marathon, not that he wrote his plays. The free man is a warrior, and only a man of war is a real man. We must look to their lives and exploits for inspiration and anticipate with great enthusiasm that such life will return. I'm afraid that, in the end, the examples of ancient men of strong hand, ancient men of power, will be very discouraging to many of you. Because you can't easily replicate their achievements and power in our time, and also, many of you are actually sissies compared to them, in your blood. But I think it's good for all of us to remember we're panty-wearers compared to them. Also, while you may not be able to emulate them in every way, because the age we live in is one of total repression, you can still take some inspiration from their examples, and try to live the same in some way...try to live according to a Bronze Age Mindset. You must not misunderstand this. This is not self-help book and I can't help you with how to live—no one can. I am concerned with the subjection of life and the suffocation of vitality. I hope to show you that things don't need to be this way, and that you don't need to limit yourself to small things. Above all you must reach for the great aim, physical and military independence. Only the warrior is a free man. The only right government is military government, and every other form is both hypocritical and destructive of true freedom. You must aim high! Band with your friends on the way of power and know that nothing has the right to stop you, and nothing can stop you! I say this especially to the military men and those who will become. Some time ago I spoke with another frog about Generalissimo Alfredo Stroessner. He was dictator of Paraguay for forty years. He went to sleep at one in the morning and got up at 4 AM; aside from this he took a two hour siesta in the afternoon (this is before air conditioning, and siesta is a necessity in tropical places). The entire day he worked relentlessly for his country and to keep down the vicious and Satanic communist sect that would have massacred his people—but he also did this for his own glory! The frog says to me, yes this drive is admirable but you have to be *specific:* You can't encourage people to strive like this to succeed at World of Warcraft, or at their career as an interior designer, there's no honor in that. I agree! But when you look at those ages in which life is ascending, the great vitality of their blood is the same as the great aim for which they reach. And although we live in the most debased of all ages, it's still possible, as you will see, to break this Babylon and have the eternal fire of youth surge you to the heights of power. In your own life you can break their power and ascend to a chaos of joy and destruction. And in our future I already see like faint image far on horizon of vast ocean in violet evening—I see the islands of Hyperborea, on the edge of this Leviathan, where we will be able to establish new outposts and subdue this great beast from the outside.

50

Imagine a Mitt Romney, but different...a Romney who actually was capable of acting like he looks, and was worthy of his looks. Imagine a younger Romney who rouses the nation to a new war, against India, through power of charisma and speech alone. Then he leave on ship to head the armies conquering India. But then come rumors that Mitt ran a Black Mass Satanist dinner in New York. Also, people awaken one day and find that someone defaced the Holocaust Museum and the Lincoln Memorial... rumors spread that it is Mitt and his friends, in preparation to overthrow the government. So he is recalled from his command to stand trial. Instead of returning, Mitt runs to Russia where he becomes a major advisor to Putin. Soon though, he finally has to leave in a great hurry when it is discovered he's been banging Putin's wife in secret. He runs to China where, again, he miraculously becomes a major political force and advisor, adopting Chinese customs and language with ease. After some time he leaves China and ends up living in Afghanistan with the tribesmen as one of them, in one of their mud fortresses, where he is finally found by American special forces and he goes out fighting, charging them repeatedly with machine gun in his glorious black-and-gold armor and Dune-like headset. Exactly such, and more, was the life of the ancient Alcibiades from Athens. How inconceivable! Even as versatile and flashy a man as Trump is very far from this possibility in our time, though he at least makes such a type somehow believable. There's nothing like it in almost any other era of history. Someone like Talleyrand is famous for switching from the monarchy, to the republic, to Napoleon, and back, being somewhat successful under different forms of government, and that's rare enough to make him famous. But that was all within one country. Alcibiades' achievement is made all the more amazing by the fact that different cultures at that time were actually different, their ways of life entirely alien to one another, and yet he excelled everywhere. I believe this is because in Athens, where he grew up, he picked the god of erotic passion as his patron. He was very beautiful youth, admired and pursued by all the men and women. He rejected the advances of the Pelasgian pedo-pervert Socrates, a story that Plato then inverted and twisted like the lying cunt and Phoenician-asskisser that he was. Alcibiades excelled in athletics and at skrewl he refused to play the flute because it made your cheeks look puffed up and ridiculous. Other boys followed him, considering that the harp is noble, but playing the flute in music is something for slaves and cocksuckers. As he grew in power, his shield had Eros with a thunderbolt on it, and this scandalized the older men. In such way he showed that he was a disciple of the irrepressible life force, a devotee of the young god of sexual passion and total destruction; he showed that no law or word of man would stand in his way! In the beginning was the word?? NO! In the beginning was the demonic fire that bursts out in men like Alcibiades and lays low the cities of men and exposes all their nonsense! Such men are sent by nature to chastise us and be our Nemesis. They are the great cleansing. His story is told by Thucydides and Plutarch, though you must know the latter is a famous liar. But I think there must be someone as colorful as Alcibiades among you.

The mystery of *rigor mortis* is very revealing! Why is dead flesh rigid? But study was made where they put dead rigid flesh into bath of ATP, the master of energy for cells, and the muscles softened and relaxed. The physiologically energetic state is the relaxed state. Flesh that is either rigid or loose is spent, but energetic biomatter vibrates in a ready repose: you see in the glowing skin of very healthy young people this relaxed suppleness in flesh, like Pietro Boselli. I've written letter to him, to ask him to allow dozens of nubile women to touch his soft, glowing, full and rubbery-like vibrating skin, all in public. The modern world exhausts and in doing so it makes everything rigid or turns it into a diffuse blob. Physiologically it promotes the stressors, estrogen, serotonin, hyperventilation, over-excitation, the hallmarks of energetic exhaustion. Loss of structure, form and differentiation follows, which was the intention. There follows on this also a spiritual and intellectual rigidity, the orientation of the ideologue, of the social activist, but also of all our intellectual class right and left, as of those who work in the corporate world and in most of the military. They're stiff and constrained because, in short, they live in *utter fear,* fear that they will lose something. They have very little to lose, but they live in this fear anyway and this is why when there is a question of potential gain or, worse for them, potential loss, they react with desperation, they freeze in terror and hyperventilate. Our politicians are all like this, and quiver in fear of the spanking hand. Everyone was already so tired of their robotic platitudes, that they repeat out of timidity and because they're all owned; which is why a man like Trump, who seems *not to care,* and to find joy in this flouting and energy in this outrageous loosening—he seduces. The modern world is a killjoy, in short. But the ancient Greeks were quite different, and different also from the over-serious stuffy men with English accents who play them in period dramas. What they admired was a carelessness and freedom from constraint that would shock us, and that upsets especially the dour leftist and the conservative role-player. There was a Hippocleides from Athens, said to be one of the most beautiful youths: Herodotus tells this famous story of a man admired by all the world of the time. He went, with dozens of other youths from various Greek cities, to try to marry the daughter of a very important and rich autocrat in Sicily. This man decided to test out the suitors, to find which would be the best husband for his daughter: he put them up for a time, treating them with lavish parties while he tested them in feats of athletics, wit, conversation, and other abilities. It's a sign of this people's greatness that marriages weren't conceived purely as political or financial alliances, but that their aristocracy paid attention to biological quality in pairings. Very few nations have the freedom from the fear I speak of; only a few peoples have had the sense to raise their snouts from the ground, look to the stars, and consider something other than the utility of immediate advantage in marriage and children. The way our own elite today marries and pairs off, by the way, is anything but "eugenic": two over-the-hill spent people in their thirties marrying for "practical" reasons...this doesn't give rise to strong children. The bodies of middle-aged people nauseate me, and I assure you, they bring nausea to nature as well. In any case, Hippocleides was becoming the favorite of the father, for all his great qualities, his illustrious lineage, his looks and his charm in conversation. At the last party, however, Hippocleides got drunk and decided to start dancing on the table. Then he started to dance upside down, on his arms, moving his legs around! Well, you know that men then didn't wear the ridiculous constraining clothmo clothes we wear today, such as pants, so the father was offended at the show. He said, "Hippocleides you have just danced yourself out of a marriage" ...but the answer was "Hippocleides doesn't care." In this one phrase you have the whole attitude of this beautiful, reckless piratical aristocracy that colonized and conquered their known world. It's an attitude that upsets all the moralfags of our time, of the left and right. Hippocleides went there to have a good time, to display and use his powers and excellences and biological superiority—but these two things are the same! He didn't care about the gain or loss of a wife. He didn't go to act like a meek, beaten male ready to dance to some sclerotic's tune. He was as careless of his own property as of others'—this is what Tacitus says also about the most noble men among the Germanic tribes, who lived only for the joy of war and battle. *This* is what the great among the Greeks admired. Another story shows you the same thing: it is also the attitude of Diogenes the Cynic. When Alexander the Great came before his bathtub and asked him what he would want most of all in the world, Diogenes told him to get out of the way, stop blocking the sun...he was just trying to catch some rays! Now compare that to one of our slavish intellectuals and philosophers, and how their meager spirits would huff and puff at the approach of even a mid-level constipated bureaucrat—how distinguished! The *honor!* Alexander said that if he had not been Alexander, he would wish to have been

Diogenes. I don't know if I can recommend for you to be like Diogenes or Hippocleides. It's hard, maybe you have to be born that way. I can tell you it's a better thing to aspire to, divine carelessness that comes from embracing the life force, and that this is what this great people loved. Anything truly great must have some of this divine carelessness. Didn't the Christians also believe in "give us but our daily bread"—implying that this is enough and you shouldn't worry about anything else, even for the week? Nietzsche say good things about poverty, independence, and being of good cheer. And these were very poor men: but the sons of God need nothing more!

52

Schopenhauer explains the carelessness and joyful frivolity of women by the fact that they live in and for the genius of the species. Although unconscious of it, they are full of its boundless aims that reach far beyond the individual, with his petty anxieties and cares: the coming of the next generation is the most serious matter. They live in the species. In them the species rejuvenates itself. It goes without saying I'm talking of women in the best case, and most specimens are botched. Why are they botched though? They've been taught to hate their own natures and instincts, and in some cases these instincts have been warped or BUTTHEXXED into something else: they've been as a wit recently put it Bernankefied up the ass. Modern women have given up this great advantage, so they can become neurotic copies of gay desk-workers. They've abandoned the great power endowed in their blood. If you don't believe me, remember a carrier pigeon that *knows* the way…surely he would lose his way if he saw a map and had to think about it. What comes from the blood is best. But it's hard to hear this call of instinct today, because you're taught to distrust it. Abandoning yourself to instinct, once one has a discipline and practice through the body, a man can pass over a chasm on a tightrope with a sure step: the left *talks* much about letting loose, about no longer being repressed. If they only understood what this really meant! I will show you men who really didn't have any hangups, who weren't repressed at all. One name was Clearchus, and he was a Spartan general. He was sent by Sparta to city of Byzantium by mouth of Black Sea. They had asked for help. He came there as military advisor, but soon no longer answered to Sparta: he used his power and contrived to invite the prominent men, the senators and the rich of the city to a meeting where they were then hung by the neck. He took their property and took the prize of sovereignty in this place! After Sparta sent an army to dislodge him, he put up a great resistance in difficult battle but was defeated. Then Clearchus managed to escape while the city was besieged; by night he sneaked away in a ship with the treasure, from a neighboring city that he had also taken over. Eventually he fled to Persia. But in Persia he didn't just enjoy his riches, which he had won by the power of his hand. This man was possessed by the passion for war and adventure. He put out a call for many mercenaries from all over the Greek world, and led this army through many bold enterprises in the wilds of Thrace and the middle of the Persian Empire where, however, he died because of treachery—here he was careless…you must be careful and know how to use the fox as well as the lion in you! I tell you of another man, praised by Machiavelli as a guide for life, a kind of life coach. He talks about a man, Agathocles, from the ancient city

Syracuse, a Greek city in Sicily. This man rose from humble beginnings, through the ranks of the army, because of his great bravery in battle and his astute mind planning stratagems and ambush. Eventually he was appointed top general in the city where, again, totally uninhibited and unencumbered, he invited the full senate and all the notables to a meeting, where his soldiers killed them all. He took the prize of power in this city. Then with many struggles he defeated the Carthaginians who were harassing the Greeks in Sicily, by landing in Africa and giving them bloody nose. He ruled securely and in great glory. I tell you these stories because they show the lives of two men who were similar, who knew how to really let loose, who weren't held back by petty inhibitions. These are men who really knew how to enjoy their freedom, and who weren't limited by the opinions of others. What was slogan of last decade in America? Yes you *can!* This is slogan of last decade in America, at least, and I see no reason why you shouldn't take this idea to its conclusions—after all, no one of the very moral wise men who rule that country saw anything wrong with that slogan. Surely they must want you to have "internalized" it. Please remember that these small people like Bill Gates, Zuckerface, and Bezos are entirely dependent men. They can't really do with their wealth what you think they can...for example, they could never just kill a man and take his wife, but even the ruler of the smallest African country has this power, this true wealth. When your happiness and wealth depends on the force of arms of another, you're not really your own man...nor can you enjoy the greatest delights in life. Clearchus and Agathocles knew this: they show you one of the ways out; they're really authentic men who went their own way! Yes you *can!*

53

The pirate and the fortress— "Work was never pleasure for me, nor homekeeping thrift, which feeds good children. But to me oared ships were pleasure, and war, and well-glinted spears and arrow." So speaks Odysseus, playing the pirate. This is motto and life of the pirate. Do you understand what pirate is? Many times I'm asked, why the Bronze Age? Because it's the heroic age you see in *Iliad* and *Odyssey,* yes, but don't forget what hero really means. Thucydides says the men of that time enjoyed piracy, and saw nothing wrong with it, and this is true. And what is the pirate but the original form of the free man and of all ascending life! How pathetic, when you are told now about "living life," or "having a life"—these people know nothing about what true life means. Compare the intensity of Alcibiades, that super-pirate, or of what I am about to describe here, to the "life" you're encouraged to "have" today. How worthless the vaunting of these anxious creatures who live on pharmaceuticals, cheap wine, the rancid fart-fumes of status and approval they beg from each other. Schopenhauer says that at some point in the past all animals were herbivores, but then some species decided to take its own life in its jaws, to *risk itself,* and with great daring become a beast of prey, living off the hunt. The predator is always the more intelligent animal. In every decision to become a hunter or pirate, a man or a people is showing great daring and embarking on great freedom. Hero is not slave to the many, who sacrifices himself for them; the common man is awed by this kind of "sacrifice," because they would never do this for themselves or others. But this is hero reduced to faithful dog. Wolf seeks not to "sacrifice" anything, but to discharge its powers over territory. We take the wolves and lions and leopards from among us when pups and break them with false ideas, vicious conditioning, and lately, drugs that would have lobotomized a da Vinci, an Alexander, a Frederick the Great out of existence in his youth. Then the energy that remains to them is channeled into mindless work for money. Labor and commerce are the ways to subject you to mere life and its preservation: when the superior are corrupted to a life of work and finance, they slowly move for their own destruction in the long run. I could say leisure is the source of all great things. The preservation of life is tedious; freedom from its demands is needed for all high science, art, and literature as well, and also all beautiful living, all adventures, all development of your body to the heights of beauty. One of the reasons the modern world has no great culture is because the sons of the rich have such bad conscience about not working, they all strive the same as others to climb on top of each other in normie jobs. Just fifty years ago most used to list "sportsman" as their main profession; that was in a recent time with slightly more beauty and more art. But...but...it is wrong to look at this aspect of life, because it assumes we have more familiarity with it than we do. It's not just that we don't "deserve" to have a higher culture, although it's that as well, but that the purpose of such a thing is completely alien to us. From the point of view of real culture and refinement we're as barbaric as the most obscure herd of the Khwarezm where the women scratch their pubes in public...we're just more tame and insipid than they were. So when I mention leisure, don't imagine I mean by it what you mean by it. It's not just leisure, you don't need just leisure for higher life, but specifically leisure for preparation for *war*. To escape the subjection of our time, you can't really look to science or art any longer: you have forgotten their purpose. They've been defanged and almost all participation in these today amounts to a kind of cargo-cultism. Who can even think of a true scientist or artist among us? I think there is maybe a century since one existed. Just see how Cellini crafted his Perseus, in what frame of mind he was, and how foreign this is from our "artist" diddlers. Paglia says the artist is an obsessive, with a mind close to that of a stalker or serial killer, and she is right: look at monomania of Newton, or character of people like Balzac or Baudelaire. Violent Spergs and obsessives. Our diddlers are diddlers because they lack all intensity and all faith in themselves and what they do. They're not even nihilists, they lack all conviction in nihilism too: they just lack intensity, they're pissed dry. This is why in this book I don't promote for you the life of the scientist, or artist, or writer, because in our age these degenerate to hobbies and ways to pass the time, and there's no value in this. People who promote these things, without really having a reason to, are just doing this to make you harmless and to advertise to others in media or elsewhere that, they too, are harmless. What past ages understood by leisure is very different from what we understand. Should robots relieve mankind of labor, there won't be any flowering of the intellect or the arts or sciences. It's not enough not be free from work, because the retired and the NEET's are like this, as well as most academics and many others, but all do nothing that's worthwhile. They've been reduced to a constrained and dependent state, and this is the problem. Constrained and dependent people don't have real thoughts: for same reason that nations without manufacturing don't really understand anymore what "innovation" and invention was for in the first place. So our science and technology too is just more diddling. Cervantes completed Don Quixote while in jail, Spinoza was a lens-grinder, Diogenes was homeless, and many other great things were done by people who were poorer or in direr straits materially than people today. And yet one can't deny that the life of the average American is that of an overworked, over-stressed slave: but the rest that would come from relieving him of that would be just that, simple rest, if it doesn't also come with manliness and sovereignty. There is no substitute for freedom and power—not even the feeling of freedom of power is a substitute for the real thing. The pirate, the true warrior—not the modern soldier in subjection to a high brass eunuch—is the only free man, and it is this freedom, the primal freedom of the Bronze Age that some must recapture before anything else can be done. Listen to what Tacitus says of the ancient Germans: they preferred to win through battle the things of life, and considered it mean and petty to work the land and sweat and toil rather than to get their living by their spears and by risking their blood. They otherwise spent much of their time in feasts and idleness. The noblest youths among them, if their tribe was at peace, would go to other tribes to seek out wars, because lack of adventure was odious to their race, and only through risking blood did they win distinction. This was also attitude of the medieval knight, the *chevalier,* the *Rittern,* the riders who considered the life of the serf, of the community, to be mean and dirty, worthy of slaves and low-castes and women: they were always ready to ride away to new things and new adventures of glory and danger. So you see, it's not enough to say "such people were freed from caring for the necessities of life; they had leisure." It was leisure of a very specific type. The Roman aristocracy, as Nietzsche says, had the motto *otium et bellum,* leisure and war, these being the only right ways of life for a man of power and freedom. In Celine's *Journey to the End of the Night* I think he says at one point that his landlady, otherwise a modest woman, had an aristocratic contempt for labor; this was but an idle vestige and he makes fun of it. By his time, the last flower of the Aryan aristocracy had been extinguished, as Nietzsche says: in French Revolution, a mass revolt of racial slaves that remade Europe and took it on the downward path. Then there was another peripheral aboriginal revolt in 1917, that plunged Europe into a civil war from which it still hasn't recovered. But in Celine's book the main character, in his restless seeking in this trash world...he was looking for that hidden key, the true freedom into the expanse of open space that he could conquer. Where to find the frontier? There are many places, but path is not easy. In the nations, leisure from the slave state must be secured, and this leisure must immediately be used in preparation for war. In Greek city the man of power spent his time in the hunt, at the gymnasium, in the study of military history and strategy, in every way making himself ready for war. Many think of the Greek age, when they think of its spirit, they think of a kind of solidarity and soldierly order quite different from what I talk about here...they think of the line of hoplites, and their discipline. They think of this age as one where the individual subsumed himself to the city and its laws, to the discipline of the ranks: and they connect this seeming egalitarianism to the practice of democracy in our time. In this way they want to flatter themselves. Modern man is then called on to make a similar "sacrifice," and blamed for his selfishness. This is confused. In beginning the hoplite, the man who fought with heavy round shield, tall spike, and heavy armor, he did not come as a "tool" of the republic or a democracy, the way modern soldiers are tools of the slave state. If you want to see what the spirit of the Bronze Age is, you look to ancient drinking song, at the mess halls of Crete and Sparta: "This is my wealth: my spear and my shield. With this I trample sweet wine from the vine. With this I am called master of serfs. Those who do not dare to have spear and sword, and fine leather shield to protect skin, all cower at my knee and submit, calling me master and great king." This was real song: a popular drinking song among the ruling men. Such formed small companies of adventurers who, early on, took over the state away from the mounted aristocracy—themselves equally piratical predators. Some time *after* they took over a state and established themselves as its rulers, they then "submitted" themselves to the rigors and discipline of a strict training program. But only in the sense that an athlete enters training in a team, specifically for making himself strong and ready for a task, and never losing sight of that specific task. When we see the Greek cities at their heights in the classical era for which we know this culture, ruled either by aristocracies or in some cases democracies, we see cities where *such men* have taken over and built a state *for themselves,* and for the purposes of training for battle and supremacy in battle. That same haughtiness and lust for physical power that you see in the song, that never left them. In the case of democracy the only difference is that the sailors are added also to the ruling assembly of armed men. And you can understand then the meaning of this ancient "public-spiritedness," which isn't that at all, but free men accepting the rigors of training together so they can preserve their freedom by force against equally haughty and hostile outsiders and against racial subordinates at home. Any "racial" unity of the Greeks was therefore only the organic unity of culture or language, but never became political: such people would never tolerate losing the sovereignty in the states they and their recent ancestors had established to protect *their* freedom and space to move. But to draw any parallels to our time is absurd: these men would have never submitted to abstractions like "human rights," or "equality," or "the people" as some kind of amorphous entity encompassing the inhabitants of the territory or city in general. They would have rightly seen this as pure slavery, which is our condition today: no real man would ever accept the legitimacy of such an entity, which for all practical purposes means you must, for entirely imaginary reasons, defer to the opinion of slaves, aliens, fat childless women, and others who have no share in the actual physical power. How is it possible for all to have an equal share in the state and a full demand on its resources, when they in fact possess no actual physical force: and if you think this question through, you will understand also the nature of our subjection in this time. Because it is not these people who are at fault, but a hidden power that uses them as a pretext. Modern "democracy" is totalitarian and vicious, and tries to subject the best to the rule of the heaps of biological refuse and most especially to the rule of those who can stir them up. The military men who constitute its external defense and its internal police forces should in principle never accept this condition. That they do is a great question mark: how is it possible? To what end, and how did they agree to this? What's in it for them? The ancient life that I describe here, the Bronze Age mindset, is one of complete freedom and power.

There is a hidden path for you also that remains...behind the marketplace, it begins in the thickets of small woods....it winds up many steep paths toward the high mountain air, to life in the ascent, uncorrupted by the miasma of the yeast man and the toilets in the river valleys....the life on Jason's *Argo* can be reclaimed...and by some few in the modern world, it has been....

54

Greek Friendship—You think maybe I promote the ruthlessness of a machine politician with tuna-stained brown sportcoat, or a petty office intriguer, or catty interior designer with upward lilting voice who backstabs his colleagues to get contract. Fools, you think I'm here to promote a "way of life" or morality! No principles or ideas are of any use today, all will be retooled and taken over by people like these. Self-help is completely useless, and not what this book is about: rather, I would like most to go toward self-destruction and to be rid of them. I only care about very few who, being constrained in their predatory nature by this open-air zoo, must look to the past to understand what is possible. I want to give encouragement to some who *are* a certain way, in their blood, and to encourage them to become the purifying hand of nature. Among your instincts you will find the longing for strong friendships, that the modern evil tries to snuff out. And they have good reason to try this, because every great thing in the past was done through strong friendships between two men, or brotherhoods of men, and this includes all great political things, all acts of political freedom and power. The modern zoo wants you instead to be a weak and isolated "individual." In most Greek cities there were the aristocratic clubs or fraternities, which were always places of great plans, great ideas and spiritual ferment. Here were made great political plans, plans of colonization and exploration of new lands and new cities, plans of conquest, actions against the designs of tyrants and plebs. Where is your bulwark today against Babylon, when all this has been made illegal for you? In life of Cellini you see how different is a real free man: when insulted, or when one of his friends or family is hurt, he gathers fifty *bravos* for a raid on the enemy, something impossible in our states today, not only because of the immense power of the evil that suffocates, but also because you have no such friends who could or would help you. A brotherhood of men in this form is the foundation of all higher life in general: there is a certain madness, an enthusiasm that exists also in a community of true scientists or artists, that follows this same pattern. It is totally forbidden in our time: it's totally absent in universities, which is where science has been sequestered. But what fate can science have here?

Everything in corporate labs, in universities, as in government labs, and at the military and intelligence facilities that still carry out some scientific tasks...everything militates to crush the spirit of science. The dedication, severity, focus and enthusiasm necessary to sustain true scientific enterprise are forbidden because they make women and weaklings uncomfortable: the presence of "lactation rooms," and an environment where such rooms could even be built...the suppression of vigorous debate, the promotion of an "unhostile environment" of petty chitchat and chumminess, the subjection of scientists to administrators, human resources cunts with fibromyalgia, to the crushing banality of everydayness, all of this reduces the young scientist to domestic muck again and destroys his aspirations and will. The assault is very heavy in Silicon Valley and other holdouts of research as well where, however, there wasn't any serious innovation being done in the first place: already technology had been reduced to the development of dick pic apps for adolescents. Science has long ago ceased and been castrated... Will it be born again? The cleansing barbarism that I talk about here must first sweep the world: no science is possible any longer, nor anything else, in a place where all spheres of life have been submerged into the great mother of the Yeast. But this isn't really about science or art, I say again, you're very far from understanding what those are even supposed to do in the first place. Do you know how for Greek all higher aspirations went into strong friendship between two men who together dedicated themselves to a higher task? In Thebes, Epaminondas and Pelopidas reformed the state, and established a democracy based on the Pythagorean sect—that last part not important. They believed in some peculiar things, like reincarnation, the veneration of the "left side" and also of beans and other legumes, which I don't understand so well. But it was they who established the famous "Sacred Band," the elite military unit that broke the power of Sparta. This group was formed of close friends, and you will always have too much love and compassion for a real friend to waiver in courage in front of him—but I doubt you understand what such friendship means or that you ever had such friend! In Athens the two friends Harmodius and Aristogeiton put down the tyranny through their schemes and their bravery: this is, you know, why all tyrants and totalitarians are suspicious of strong friendships between men. Most of all this is feared by the middle-aged lesbos and defectives that are used as guards by our prison-states. And yes, I know the rumors that these friendships were sexual, but I believe this is misunderstanding and exaggeration promoted by the homonerds of our time, for reasons I will explain later. The model for all such friendships was that between Achilles and Patroclus: Homer never hints such friendship was sexual. It is only out of the poverty of our imagination that we think it was, because we can't conceive of such intense love between friends without some carnal or material benefit in play. It was out of his friendship for Patroclus that Achilles embarked on his great rampage: it was for the sake of his friend that he would not tolerate living a long and inglorious life at home...he chose instead a short and glorious one, and a violent death full of promise and beauty. Friends can spur you to this! How shameful to drag out life like a dog and die overseen by strangers in a hospital, who hate you, rather than to die in the prime of your youth, for the sake of your friend, and to leave behind a beautiful corpse! The original form for all this was the divine pair of charioteers: Castor and Pollux, or for the Aryans it was the Ashvin twins, and for the Saxons it was Horst and Hengist, the pair of the chariot driver and the archer—do you understand this is the real root of all the higher aspirations of Europe? The charioteers who took over Europe around 1500 BC depended on this close bond between two men for its military organization; and probably this people itself had its ultimate origins in friendships of this kind. The Spartan state, in any case, entirely depended in its education of youth on this pairing of two friends, as knight and squire. It was this conquering aristocracy that really made Europe stand out from the morass that the rest of the world has always been stuck in... And for the Greeks, and all great men of the Bronze Age and not just the Greeks, friendship wasn't just a way to "temper" the lust for power and adventure that some of you will surely embrace, but an absolute prerequisite for it. It is most of all *not* a duty. Friendship is a social relation of a kind that is beyond all "ethics," you see, and if you ever think of it in terms of ethics you misunderstand it. It is a great pleasure between two, very different from sexual pleasure between man and woman, but of the same species, in that it is pleasant, and never feels like "ethics," which is for cows. There have been a few attempts in our age to replenish this form of friendship, for example Montaigne's famous essay. There have been other attempts as well, you find some nice words on friendship in Nietzsche in *Zarathustra*, and then most of all there are the modern scouting movements, that come from Germany and from this same spirit. The first movement like this was called the Wandervogel, but there were various others, all based on the experience of nature, the promotion of camaraderie and of nationalism. This included the Jewish youth guard movements that became Zionists, the Boy Scouts and others in America of course. Among the Jews, the promotion of this kind of camaraderie and friendship was a great miracle in the early 20th Century, because it so much went against their culture of the cramped *shtetl*, of nerds dominated by women and old people and by fear. It was a great act of self-overcoming for them, and many are right that in some sense the creation of Israel is the most "anti-Semitic" act ever conceived. It is, in any case, a great model for others to show that reestablishment of antiquity is fully possible, although there is no real reason why Americans or Europeans should have any regard for the welfare of this country. In their case too, however, by our time that spirit of piracy is long gone, and they've gone so soft that on the streets of Tel Aviv you have Yemeni "Jewish" bluegums with Rasta style feeling up Ashkenazi girls, and in general a feeling of torpor. The condition of other modern nations is worse. In our time friendship is made illegal between boys in school, real fraternities are for all purposes banned, and the scouting movements are forced to accept women—and women are destructive entirely of any great friendship. In private life, friendship among isolated and defeated modern males is unheard of. Men are deluded into thinking their wife can also be their best friend (and this, of course, also makes their wives lose respect for them). Then also so many are rightly afraid of the way such relations have been sexualized between men and are never sure if a prospective friend has sexual intentions...at the same time as all this goes on, gays act out a domesticized

134

and castrated parody of friendship. Where to recover true friendship then? In this case though, more than in others, how could they stop you, if you only learned to listen to instinct and follow the pleasure of desires? There's nothing in principle that the state can do to stop you, if you should give yourself over to real friendship. All of the things I've said are a kind of conditioning, a very strong conditioning, but it's all a form of psychological control that should in principle be easy to break. All you need to do is give in to desire for great things. The true foundation of the Bronze Age, of the age of great adventures...such a thing is a matter of the blood and spirit and for those few among you who are suited to it, it should be as easy to recover as the carelessness that comes from filling yourself with the fire of the life-force. You must only embrace your own instincts with abandon and understand that in common dedication to a higher cause, a great friend is invaluable because you spur each other on and keep guard on each other in the mission.

55

Superman mindset—inside every noble Greek was an unquenchable lust for power, and this means power to become lord over life and death in your state. It's hard to understand what this means from looking around today, because there's nothing like it from the big examples you might have heard. Many of you might think of dictators in North Korea or some public lavatory of the world, or of the great total states of the last century, but you'd be wrong. These men weren't really free or powerful, in many ways they were hostage to their own security services. Someone like

Stalin was trapped in a stream of events where his freedom to operate existed only in the realm of murder, and murder alone, and any small step outside of this would mean his doom. Ideology is so tiresome! These are "systems" of control that call on the mobilization of the entire society; and the demands of this control far outweigh the capabilities of a single man. In a monarchy he could delegate these tasks to ministers and concern himself with other projects, but someone like Stalin or Mao can't really do that. You must understand that all true greatness is parasitic on matter, for example the brain and nervous system are parasitic on the body: for anything good to happen the capacity of the hegemon must exceed the demands made on it for attention, management and control. The analogy here would be a body with the lower organs so large and powerful, their demands for control so overwhelming, that the brain would be barely equal to the task and would remain entirely in their service, although ruling or tyrannizing over them. That is the kind of "modern dictator" you know about. And the types of men that are drawn into this today are also quite different, they are the kind of ideological martinet you meet every day among those who are "public spirited" and into "public service." It's a kind of very aggressive schoolmarm type. This is a lower kind of creature. What I'm talking about is entirely different from public service, but seeks to live like a parasite on the state and on the substance of its various factions, to pursue quite different interests and desires. They have interests alien to yours. In the modern world this condition isn't approached by dictators of totalitarian states, but certain others I will describe soon. In fact the great totalitarian states you know about weren't that different from our own, or the "liberal democracies": we live in the same kind of state, only that it is more prosperous and the viciousness of the power is indirect and hidden. But it is no less monstrous. If anyone is free, it certainly isn't anyone you see or know about. No Greek that I talk about, in any case, would have enjoyed being the gofer of the national security and industrial state and its thousands of demands. Such men saw the prize of sovereignty as a means...a perch from where they could remain watchful over the state and of territory far outside it, and swoop down like eagle for the prize; in one swoop the king of birds catches its bloody prey in fast talons. They were true *artistes*: take, for example, Periander of Corinth. This man's name means literally "superman." At no point in his life as king of Corinth did he restrain his lust for the darkest paths: it is said he copulated with his mother, that he violated his wife's corpse, and much worse. He had all the boys on the island Corcyra castrated. And, having done all this, he was memorialized as one of the Sages, or Geniuses of the ancient world. A philosopher and a poet, he wrote an epic on the mysteries of nature... that showed themselves to him alone on afternoons when the long shadows make the blue-green shores of those seas whisper to ears ready to hear. He supported also the art and philosophy of others in the state, but only out of a careless generosity: I was there at his court, I played the harp and he once threw a well-used courtesan in my lap with a gesture of disdain. It is true that he established his city as a great trading outpost, bringing great wealth. He also built the first railroad in history—a kind of way to transport goods across the isthmus of Corinth; at the time a great innovation. He did many other such things...he established colonies abroad, he built temples, he chastised the nobles and raised up the middle classes, but you must forgive these acts, or rather, not misunderstand them. He never did any of this "for the good," out of duty or necessity, but rather these actions flowed from those we consider vices, as a kind of excess. Everything came from his instincts to conquer and expand the domain of his action. Born to power in his state, he could have chosen a middle course. If he had excessively enjoyed honors...or prestige...or security. These were his to have, and easily. The great danger for a house passes once the son is able to succeed the father in seat of king. But he gave all this up, for really no reason. He chose a path of adventure, but ...he chose even a path of sorrow. In all he did, there was a kind of artistic sorrow and grotesque misfortune, that he seemed to want to bring on himself...to make life interesting, or so he could overcome even *this* latest outrage. He killed his own wife, and I know why. She was pregnant, and though he had copulated with her, in a dream he received word that during the act a small snake had become attached to his member. And that a monster would be born. Then it's said that his son was murdered by those same people from Corcyra that Periander had made the subjects of his weird experiments, but that they did so because they loved the youth. But this is absurd. The real reason was that he was trying to impregnate all the women on the island. So Periander dreamt he would become progenitor of a "brood of snakes." He only ever saw political office as a means to self-overcoming and self-perfection, as a way to turn himself into a living work of art. From this came for the citizens much good and also much bad. It has to be expected that such men will appear as monsters to others. In any case, the things he did were hardly the worst. One other man I can think of, a tyrant or a king, have it what you will, he married off the women of his state to slaves: through this overturning of values, that he learned from Plato, he secured his infamy and power. Do you understand what Plato's *Republic* means? It is a formula for such men to unleash their complete madness on the world. It teaches them certain tricks to expand the domain of their struggle for self-perfection into every area of social life. Plato himself says that the secret desire of every Greek was to become a tyrant, and Nietzsche understands all the greatness of that people, their exploration of the seas and limits of the world, their foundation of the arts and sciences...all of this as just an extension of this secret desire in the heart of every noble Greek. It was the secret desire also in the heart of the great French artists, and it is simply put, *the* unlearnable desire behind all great things. If you have it you must by no means restrain it. This is because human nature is feeble and easily led astray, and only when driven by this kind of monstrous and single-minded obsession for the heights of power can it find the motivation to overcome the lying, dirty ape in us. A certain distance too from oneself is necessary. A "clinical" eye in regards to oneself, one's faults, is required for this mindset. In our time this can be achieved in part by embracing spirit of true science, whereas for man of Bronze Age it was easy to embrace because he saw things that happened to him, including the great motions of the spirit, the feelings that troubled him, as instantiations of various gods, for which *he was not responsible,* and which he could therefore judge and evaluate externally. His view was, however, correct. For this reason when you see men like Periander you have to understand their special quest wasn't one

139

where they try to accomplish "the public good," nor was it some worthless desire to dominate others or exert will for petty satisfaction: they see others instead as tools or objects on a mission of self-overcoming. He was trying to turn himself into a work of art, his life into a replay of the great motions of the stars, or the secret passion plays of the gods. In the same way that the Greek state in general was conceived as a work of art by the citizens. Periander understood his position as king then as just another means: here science, here art could be free from all limits and could rule unhindered and embark on great experiments. And yet from all this you see something very strange…The secret desire of every Greek…the Bronze Age mindset….was to be worshiped as a god! This is the secret target to which that boundless lust for power aims! There are many other examples. Among the Spartans you find the great general Lysander. He turned the Spartans from a land power into a great navy, defeated the Athenians and ended the Peloponnesian War: then he went from city to city as a liberator, on a great tour of self-glorification. He was the first to be worshiped as a god at altars. He had searched for this his entire life, and it was the prize of his victories. There was another such unlikely man, Brasidas, a Spartan general of a generation before Lysander, of very unusual character. He liberated many cities by his force of personality and the magical charisma that emanated from his body. A Spartan and man of battle and the science of war, he nevertheless managed to win by persuasion and speech: only *such* man, with disdain for words, can really understand what speech is really for. He was type of man who, when his back is against the wall, the strong spirit in him rallies like wild boar who rages in his thick chest when he is cornered by hunters, and charges for the kill. In same way Brasidas performed best when he relieved many cities of siege. He died the most glorious death, in the middle of victorious battle, when he rushed into the thick of the enemy with his elite guard. He was worshiped as a god thereafter in the city of Amphipolis. It's not a surprise that you see men of this type of man come out of Sparta: the place that made the sternest demands on itself produced also the most brilliant men. They went rogue and easily imposed the intensity of their magic charisma on foreigners. True power needs no effort: it draws all around it like a force-field. Power of character and body attracts others in orbit as if by magic.

56

In *Iliad* you see the greatest warriors rise up to fight even the gods. When Diomedes is about to go on his great rampage, Athena the white-eyed appears to him and whispers in his ear. She reminds him of his father's great feats and breathes strength into his chest: she tells him to go fearlessly into the throng of the enemy on his chariot and in this exalted condition she draws back from his eyes the veil that had previously hidden the gods. She tells him that if that harlot Aphrodite appears, he has the power to harm her. And Diomedes does this without any fear! Even the goddess of love is laid low before the aroused might of a warrior on rampage. Achilles too in his great moment chastises the river god and makes him submit. This reflects one great truth, that in this condition of aroused spirit the true man is given the gift of heightened perception and can see things that others can't. This is what is meant by the fact that the genius sees this same world we do, but sees in it things that we can't, much like we see things that dog or ant can't. Indeed time itself entirely changes when the will is raised up to this height: the warrior in some way can be said to rise outside the stream of events in which we are held like prisoners. In this condition he appears magnified, anointed and others who are not privy to the same things begin to orbit around him physically and spiritually: in the Bible too you see in the middle of battle for Jerusalem, "the House of David shall be as God, as the angel of the Lord" before the many, who subject themselves in awe to this great gift. In same way in their moments of great glory Athena kindles on the neck and head and shoulders of the warriors a great *fire* that can be seen from far away. She does this for Diomedes and for Achilles as they let loose their strength on a wild rampage, a great bonfire explodes on their body and behind them. This is the irresistible power of charisma and strength that draws all to it like magic: for man this is no less true than it is for migratory birds on mission, for pack of wolves on the hunt, for hives of bees, in all cases the many begin to orbit around the anointed hegemon as if by magic. It's a biological compulsion, and a great good. And you must understand one thing: the end of Achilles' mission was the total destruction of the city of Troy, the fire melting the brick of its alleys, its men killed, its women and children sold into slavery. This last was held to be the right of conquerors throughout the history of the Greek world, or at least for its vital period of ascent. Thus this most humane and refined of ancient peoples found it absolutely necessary nevertheless to have this *out* for the wolfish and predatory instinct in man. War alone brought rejuvenation of their nature. When Alexander drags the body of the rulers of Tyre outside the city walls from his chariot, and circles around the city, he is copying what Achilles did to Hector when the city of Troy was annihilated. Nietzsche sees in this an excess, something unfortunate...but I tell you, he means something else. When city is destroyed its gods are destroyed: you must remember that each city had its tutelary gods and spirits for protection. The Romans, before they conquered a new city, promised the gods of that city that they would honor and respect them tenfold more than the inhabitants. When a city or culture is destroyed, gods are destroyed with it. The destruction of the cities in fire that the greatest warriors of antiquity took upon themselves was a form of divine warfare. And it was only possible because such men *knew also how to listen to the voice of the gods,* and allowed themselves to be entirely possessed by a divine madness. It imbued them with superhuman strength, and drew others into their designs by instinct. This abandon to nature and instinct—this is the Bronze Age way! And you can learn to cultivate this exalted psychosis inside you also.

57

I see no reason why, if there should be epidemics of all kinds of diseases, the same can't also be true for what we call "mental disease." And you see repetitions of this throughout history and even now: among primitives in Sudan, when they become possessed of fears that wandering Jews are spreading penis-modifying bananas, or that shaking hands can destroy your genitalia, or such things. This is funny but in all eruptions of this kind of superstition I see a divine significance and great potential. In Europe there used to be the mania called St. Vitus' Dance, and in ancient Greece the cults of Dionysus spreading the madness of maenads and turning the women into hungry, cannibalistic *sluts*. I say this in "sex-positive" way! I believe any child born of such excesses is likely to be blessed, because here the genius of the species is allowed to make the choice without any interference. This is not endorsement of anything in our time: there is nothing like this, it's just LARP'ing. You've been abandoned by the gods. Only a global orgy of fire will whet their appetites for return.

58

You make fun of "decadent" Roman Emperors? In the horror stories from Suetonius you have prototype of "monarchy gone wild," of mad emperors who use position only to satisfy arcane and criminal lusts. I don't write to defend such things, but the condemnation isn't moral—how can it be, when my reaction at reading excesses of Caligula or Nero or Tiberius is to feel a great sense of loss, or envy at what they could do that I can't? Caligula had the genius idea to form a long line of ships on the sea, put platforms on top of them, fill them with earth, so that he could fulfill a prophecy of walking on water between two points. He gathered the army on the seashore facing Britain and ordered them, instead of invading, to collect seashells. He then called this a great booty for the Roman People and the Senate and threw a few pennies at the soldiers saying "Go Happy! Go Rich!" He captured two Gauls but dressed them up in Ice-Nigger-Face to look like Teutons and then enacted an obviously transparent "hunt" to pretend he had captured them in front of the soldiers. Everyone laughed and rolled their eyes, for sure. But he was caught up in the story of his own godhood. At Rome he used to lock down the Colosseum during the hottest hours and withdraw the awnings so that the people would suffer in the heat and pregnant women wouldn't be able to leave. Sometimes he replaced the regular gladiator shows with pathetic fights between cripples and deformed animals; he would lock down the granaries to let the people go hungry for no reason at all. He was the greatest troll ever. When the Jews of Alexandria came to complain about civil war simmering in that city, he ignored their pleas and asked them why they don't eat pork. When you look at Elagabalus you see this tendency taken to its logical conclusion: this man was a trap-Emperor, and asked his doctors to give him a sex change operation. It is believed he was a devotee of Cybele, and like the insane priests of that cult...wanted to castrate himself. Instead of this, he became a prostitute inside the palace, and used to publicly give himself airs over how much he was making. Commodus became a gladiator and found great pride in his swordplay, although such things aren't so strange to imagine in our time: and they are to be welcomed! Nero was a pioneer of gay marriage. The first time he did it as the groom, and the second as the bride: he made the old senators listen as he mimicked the sounds of a young wife getting deflowered behind the doors. Of all his exploits I found most fascinating that he put on the mask of a lion and, having tied up various men and women naked in his mansion on the island, came at them with the rage of a beast and in a frenzy bit at their bodies and genitals. I don't celebrate any of this, but I think when in our age elites are accused of similar behavior...this isn't right...I think we flatter ourselves. We want to think they're a lot more interesting than they are...it's easier to think we're ruled by demons than by defectives who would normally be running a smoked-fish stand or running vodka parlors outside Minsk. We don't want to admit that we're as lame in vice and deviance as we are in greatness, and for the same reasons. You see these old wet rags of an "elite" getting arrested, and in almost every case it's for something on the level of a Pee Wee monkey-show, self-exposure in a porn cinema, masturbating themselves in front of some frigid cinema whore with leatherface and bugged out eyes, exposing their weapons of mass destruction to a Dominican maid. It's hard to understand what even goes into this kind of "decadence," but it's of a different kind from the excesses of the worst Roman Emperors, who, even when they were trannies, seem more manly and brave than our perverts. I wonder if it's not possible to think of history in entirely different way, I mean: all we think now is from point of view of *the people,* and the story goes about progress or regress with respect to how they fare; or at best how something like science or hygiene advances, or technology, or moral responsibility, or equality, or inequality, or anything else you want....advances or not. But history would look very different if pursued with eye of connoisseur for superior specimens, judging them as you would prized steers or stallions. In such case you would have to dismiss these kinds of freaks like the emperors I mentioned, and judge them defective...but for entirely different reasons. You would learn to see history from view of *life and biology...* as great bestiary...and learn what is necessary in our time also to make way for the long-lost tropics and jungle...the abode of the gods....that can return....and return........

59

I always loved the statues of the *kouroi.* I can safely say that upon viewing such statue by myself for three hours (someone let me in to look alone in museum), I was able to ejaculate without touching myself. But I had no dirty or untoward thoughts the entire time. This experience made me wonder...if it is possible to ejaculate without touching yourself, is it possible also to will yourself to death just the same, without doing anything? The *kouroi* have long story behind them, you might have heard. At first these statues were copied from Egyptian models, but they became much more realistic in the hands of the craftsman of the Archaic Greeks, also much brawnier and more muscular. The pose is still stylized and the smile they have on their face is very enigmatic, almost like you think they could crush big stone on your head, or run iron blade through your sternum and have that stoney, autistic smile unchanged while looking you in the eye. Two brothers of this type had to carry their mother to a religious feast. It is story of Kleobis and Biton, twins. She couldn't get there on her own, so they carried her on a kind of palanquin, rushing with great force up the steps to the temple. They presented her in time to the sacred procession, but both died from the great exertion. Herodotus says Solon told this story to Croesus of Lydia, who was one of the first self-made kings we know from history. Croesus took his state by force, with the help of a company of elite warriors. He was the one who made the first coins, to pay his mercs. He ruled outside all limits and pursued the way of power. In this he inspired many to similar actions. But Solon, the wise founding father of Athens you could say, a famous lawgiver, went to visit him. He asked Solon to tell him about people who lived a happy life and Solon told him this story of the brothers. The full story says that after the twins performed this great athletic feat and delivered their mother in time to the sacred feast, she asked the goddess Hera, to which she was dear, for a great reward. And the goddess gave this reward, that the twin sons would lie down in the temple for a deep sleep, and never awake. This is idea of a Greek.... of a happy life. This story confused Croesus the king, and it probably confuses you. It's strange to see how far the Greeks took aesthetic understanding of life and the world. There is no moral lesson in this story at all. Any moral lesson that you could think of, for example of duty to parents or to tradition, could have been made in different way. What's unusual here is the ending. There is just biology: it is best for the end and the acme to coincide. A beautiful death at the right time is the only key to understanding a life, its only hidden "meaning." It is a beautiful death to die after accomplishing a great feat for the glory of one's city, family and for the gods, but it's greater still to die in one's prime, at the height of your powers and at the acme of their discharge. A beautiful death in youth is a great thing, to leave behind a beautiful body, and the best study of this pursuit you find in the novels of Mishima, a real connoisseur.

60

The most glamorous Christian prince for me was always young Conradin, King of the Romans and King of Jerusalem. He was unjustly killed in Italy by usurper Charles of Anjou with the contrivance of a corrupt Pope. He came from an illustrious family. His grandfather was the emperor Frederick II Hohenstaufen, called *Stupor Mundi* and celebrated by Nietzsche. His beauty was said to be resplendent, like that of his half-brother Manfred who was holding much of Italy by force of charisma and arms while Conradin was still a small boy. Upon reaching age at thirteen or fourteen, Conradin embarked with his few but powerful knights southward to reclaim his rightful throne in Rome. He defeated the usurper and then entered the city. Riding at the head of his column of knights in all their full armor, with the imperial banners raised high—this was a glorious day, all the people came to the streets to welcome their beloved liberator and showered the procession with many flowers. The outpouring of love for this boy was like something that hadn't been seen since the age of the Empire, and this alarmed the Pope and all the sclerotic prelates as much as this boy's grandfather had, if not more. Conradin was just thirteen or fourteen, but he refused all orders to wait and never listened to the timid counsels of his advisors who tried to hold him back from his acme. He entered Rome as world-conqueror. Thereafter came a series of disasters: his army lost a great battle in the south, despite a successful first charge, and mostly through the inadequacy of some of his auxiliaries. He was captured by treachery and then Charles of Anjou, with the help of corrupt jurists, found a legal pretext to put him on trial and behead him and a friend. You might think this is very bad, and certainly it would have been better to die in the middle of battle, but much can be excused by his youth. And it must be said that he never compromised or begged for his life. His execution was so absurd and unjust that it permanently discredited Charles of Anjou, the usurper. It discredited too this kind of Papal "legalism" that must sound very familiar to you now. Still more so, it permanently discredited the aggressive Papacy that promoted a man the people of Sicily and Italy—as well as most of the German states—viewed as an arrogant, nearly-autistic, and unjust upstart. This Charles was ever driven in his life by the hatred that came from being slighted in his youth by his mother and other relatives. He was a man driven by a sclerotic lust for power and crude ambitions, where Conradin was carried by the native charisma common in his family, by his beauty, his careless courage. He was riding to seat of world-ruler purely through naïve trust in his own glamor. Know that despite all force and treachery and contrivance, all public sanctions and honors, the people will not be fooled: they know the real man of power, and can tell the difference from a deformed usurper. Charles' execution of Conradin was lamented by all Germany and much of Italy. Now the robots who run our world also want to be loved or feared, and are trembling because the people don't respect them. They too, the nations of our time, seek the return of youth, of a Conradin. It seemed to the peoples of that time a story of the promise of youth, the beauty and purity of its intentions, extirpated by the old and ugly. So that in the end the memory of the young prince was victorious. Not long after this the peoples of Sicily conspired with the House of Aragon, ruled by relatives of Conradin, and broke the power of Charles in a revolt. This was the end of idea of "universal monarchy" through the Papacy...and this was the

150

beginning of the national consciousness in Europe. The memory of Conradin was prized as the promise of beauty and youth, memorialized in epics and poetry, that rejuvenated the peoples of Europe and awoke them. Though he died without achieving his goal, he died as a martyr for Europe against Asia, and inspired the birth of the new state—the springboard of world conquest that was soon to come in the age of exploration and colonization. Christianity is a versatile faith, capable of many interpretations. I believe Conradin was the most Christian prince but also might as well have been the renewed avatar of Apollo in Europe, recalling very old memories. It was the spirit of fire and youth renewing the peoples through its magnetic power and then through the sacrifice of its blood. In moments of torpor we can always return to this spirit of the ancient Greeks as a tonic.

61

Crusaders like Cortes and Pizarro, Fernando de Soto, Drake and Raleigh, Magellan and Balboa equal in daring, intelligence, magnitude of spirit, resourcefulness and achievement any of the great men of the Greeks and Romans. The story of the heroic age of exploration remains to be told in full, and maybe one of you one day will make big book or big movies. I say also now: for those who seek to make a difference and have some artistic or visual bent, movies are *the* golden key to the minds of the many. What Mel Gibson does is worth a thousand books or "activisms" for your side. Learn to make movies, if you can, and you can start with video. In any case, there is just one great epic that tells the story in its proper form, the great poem of Camoes, a man born to piracy and high adventure. This man lost an eye in war in Ceuta against the Moor; he then lived as a brigand and vagabond in imperial Lisbon, getting into one duel and fight after another, composing poetry, getting drunk. His mother saved him from prison, but he was pressed into service in the colonial navy and army. He arrived in Goa and from there participated in many adventures, military and diplomatic, as a man of low rank but high spirits. All the while he was writing his great poem the *Lusiad,* and when he was shipwrecked off the Mekong with his Chinese girlfriend, he carried the text of this timeless work above his head to save it from the water. No one reads it anymore, and his life would make a great movie. But he is right that the voyages of these new crusaders equal any great expedition even from the myths and legends of the past. Here we have Jason's Argo made anew, and not just once, but in every one of these nations of the West. England's glory during these years might never be equaled again by any people. Even the kings of Portugal, who started the age of colonization and exploration, had English blood. The Gothic restlessness of the steppe shook in the lords of Iberia with a Titanic energy. Before the great voyage to the Orient of Vasco da Gama, spies—and I mean just one or two men—went *alone* on expeditions in Egypt and down the Red Sea, into the heart of Arabia, fearlessly, incognito, to collect information crucial for the coming expedition. Perched on the beaches of the great Eurasian mass, these men went, in just a hundred years, from sailing a few almost-rafts that they barely knew how to navigate, to explorers of new worlds and founders of global empires that lasted for centuries. You must understand how amazing this feat was: there *was* no tradition of seamanship in Portugal or Spain, let alone France or England...it all had to be done from scratch. Do you know at all to respect the sea? If you've ever traveled a ferry on even a relatively calm sea like the Adriatic, on a windy day a large modern ferry, as big as a city block...it will swing right and left. You won't be used to it. The Atlantic has waves ten feet or more as a matter of course and these men were traveling on wooden ships with 15th Century tech; you must be crazy to have no awe of this. For romance of the sea you should read Melville. Columbus is celebrated, yes, but there were others who were even greater than him, or at least his equal, and few know about them. They don't receive the glory they deserve because, first, many of the writers who could have done this were prejudiced against their strong religious faith and their piety: you see, most of the modern glorifiers of antiquity usually had an axe to grind against Christianity or the Church, so they didn't want to promote these men, or admit that the champions of the faith were the most shining exemplars of the classical man in our time. Even Nietzsche stays away from them and, in a moment of weakness, speaks nonsense about the "superiority" of the Aztecs. On the other hand, the Church has been embarrassed about these men. More than anyone else they spread its power and gospel through the world, and even before that, they saved Europe itself from the Moors and the other threats. They're the direct descendants of the crusaders who liberated Spain and other parts of Europe. The Church doesn't want to admit that once Ferdinand and Isabella cleared Spain of the enemies of Christ, God blessed that nation with a century of prosperity and pre-eminence, and gave it the foundation of world-empire. But the Church was embarrassed by them, by the *conquistadores*, by their cruelty and their pagan love of vitality and action, so it tried to disavow them while making use of their strength. So their story remains largely untold, although it's one of the peaks of history and of manly achievement. Few understand the voyages, for example, of even one of the most famous among them, Vasco da Gama and how in many ways it exceeded the feats of Columbus. This man circumnavigated Africa and found the sea route to the Indies—what Columbus had actually set out to do (or so the story goes...I believe Columbus had some secret maps...) Such voyage was attempted long before by the Phoenician Hanno, but no one knows what really came of that. The travel was difficult. When you reach a certain point of the West African coast you can't just continue to hug along it...you have to pull out to the west and swoop around—this is likely how South America was discovered. Do you know what starvation, scurvy, and tropical disease is? Do you understand tropical heat? Sure, some of you might, but know that off the West Africa coast, when a wind blows in your face it's not a relief: it's like a hairdryer going off in your face, nonstop. And yet he reached India, he found spices, he found monkey, he made the Zamorin submit with big guns. His investors made thousands of percent return. Just seven years later another conquistador returned, Almeida, with a great armada that tore a swathe of destruction along the Indian Ocean. He burned down Mombasa, though outnumbered, because of the arrogance of its Arab rulers—imagine the stench that must have wafted as far as Japan! This man defeated a huge armada of Ottomans, Arabs, Mamelukes at the Battle of Diu, to avenge the death of his son: and this was momentous time. Space itself on our world changed. The great overland routes of trade were now outflanked by the seafaring nations of western Europe, which from this moment began to dominate the Indian Ocean and the Pacific. Do you understand America had a great destiny in this design as well? When the colonists founded Jamestown, let's say there were no more than two hundred or two hundred and fifty years from that act to the time of Commodore Perry: the American people had tamed the continent and pushed their way to Asia across the seas in no time at all. It would have happened even faster if they hadn't been hampered by the domination of England...once they gained their independence their expansion was very fast (the Constitution, the ideology, the doctrine of rights, is all so much nonsense and has nothing to do with any of this...it barely all even lasted through the lifetimes of the founders of America, who were seeking merely dominion and freedom of space to expand). The great destiny of America had always been the conquest of the Far East and the domination of China, which obsessed the leading minds of that time. All of this has now been forgotten and America's great fate has been thwarted—at least for now. What do you know then of men like this, or of Afonso de Albuquerque who followed Almeida, who captured Hormuz and Muscat with seven ships, who opened the way to the Spice Islands of legend? I prefer as usual not to talk of such men: they are so far from your possibilities that the example is almost depressing. I want to *encourage* you again with someone else from this age, a man more to my taste, and more within the realm of what is possible, of what is about to become possible again. This is the brilliant right-hand-man of Cortes, Pedro de Alvarado. He was a man of knightly family from southern Spain, but had fiery red-blond hair, which amazed the Mexicas: they believed he was a child of the Sun, and called him Tonatiuh, the mane of the sun. He was of boundless courage, carelessness, and also boundless cruelty. Cortes left him in charge briefly in Tenochtitlan where he massacred all the Aztec nobles in the Great Temple during a banquet...for no reason at all. During the battles he distinguished himself by insane charges into the thick of the enemy by which he was outnumbered by hundreds to one: yet he never lost heart, he went right for their garish flower-decorated lieutenants and cut them down, striking fear into the multitude. Don't believe the lies about gunpowder. Guns were very basic at this time, and on many occasions the Spanish didn't have guns at all. The armor, the pikes, the Toledo steel blades, the discipline and know-how from decades of fighting the Moor—all of this was far more important. And above all, bravery and daring, the same that led Pizarro to take down an empire with a retinue of thirteen men. What I want to say about Alvarado, though, is this: once conquests were made, *he never stopped.* His thirst for space, for new worlds, for new conquests, was without end. In his letters you see this is his only interest. Though made governor of a huge area—the present-day states of Guatemala, of Honduras, these are his creations—he nevertheless showed no interest at all in ruling them. He squeezed them of whatever money he could, never paying any taxes back to Spain, and always planned new adventures and new conquests. This man was a born pirate: right before his death he was planning a great expedition for the conquest of China and the Spice Islands. Alvarado was a nemesis to civilization, and this is right and good. God sends such men to chastise mankind. I want you to be like this: to listen to these instincts in you. When he was put in charge of territory, Alvarado could have very easily settled down to the life of a governor; most men would. Enticed by the prestige and honor, they would play the part: then also, their vanity would fool them into thinking that they could govern well. Well, maybe you can govern well, or maybe you can't. But Alvarado *knew what he was.* And he didn't try to be more than one thing. Be one thing. Single-minded purity of purpose is true manliness. He knew he was a born beast of prey, and never pretended to be more or less than this. This self-assured sense of who he was made him insanely attractive even to the natives he oppressed and massacred: despite his cruelty, they couldn't help being drawn to his charm, his lofty manner, his outrageous magnificence. They worshiped him as a god. The other Spaniards were in awe as well. You must see that nature blesses all men who have faith in their own blood and in their instincts...nature blesses them with such magnetism. Alvarado is the avatar of our new age, and I predict this: within fifty years a hundred Alvarados will bloom from deep in the tropical bestiary of the spirit. They will sweep away the weakness of this world.

62

Bob Denard shows that the spirit of Bronze Age pirate can exist also in our age. It can flower complete and unedited. You have no excuse! This man may not be what you expect. How different he is from the pretentious bureaucrats we see, the politicians with their high-flown language, their tedious moral preaching, their careful self-positioning, timidity, and the drudgery to which they subject themselves. Men who embrace high-flown moral principle in public are usually looked down on by many regular people; they can smell the bullshit from far away. He started out as a regular soldier with the French in Vietnam, but he was court-martialed after he burned down a bar—part of a dispute, you see. Some men chimp out by writing a complaint, others by getting in a bar fight, others by burning down the building. After this he wandered around Africa, finding odd jobs in the employ of local nabobs and potentates, all of them utterly corrupt and incompetent. He said once something like, "It's important never to be 'ambitious.' Men of 'ambition' are losers. Act and feel like a winner and good things, friends, and victory will come." He took part in adventures all over Africa: coups in Benin, the Congo, secessionist movements like in Biafra (the French styling on English Nigeria) and so forth. His greatest feat was to overthrow the government of the Comoros four times. Each time France had to send special forces to the islands to dislodge him. Otherwise he would have surely become a hereditary ruler. He had many wives and won many properties by the power of his hand. At the end of his life…well…this life lasted too long. He should have died in defense of his territory, younger, and without descending into the dementia and pain that took him in old age. France repaid his service with persecution; no longer needed to fight communists in Africa, his vainglory and ferocity became a liability. Now, if you need great moral elevation, if war must be in the service of a good cause, you can consider his service in Congo, in Katanga and then against the Simba rebels. At Stanleyville he, along with only a handful of other white mercenaries, freed thousands of hostages from rape and sure massacre at the hands of the savage Simbas. In many ways he defended whatever residues of civilization remained in Africa after decolonization. In this last venture he was joined by a man of similar temperament, the Colonel "Mad Mike" Hoare. This is another great example of the modern rebirth of Bronze Age vitalism. And another example of why you're a fag. An Irish-English dandy, he was a gentleman among soldiers, but a man before being a gentleman: he remained throughout his life single-minded, brutal and cool-headed in the middle of conflicts where he was outnumbered thousands to one, swamped by the demented *zombi* hordes of the tropics. This man understood communism for what it was: the infestation of vermin he was tasked to exterminate, a biological event, not an ideological, political, or historical one. After the war in Burma he made a living working on safaris and then, like Denard, gaining experience in the service of various African governments. He led an elite unit of mercs in the Congo, and in the same operation with Denard, was responsible for relieving Stanleyville and saving a hundred nuns and missionaries from rape and torture. Thereafter he led many missions in Africa, a new frontier. He was later involved in an aborted coup on the Seychelles. Failure is not dishonorable, as long as you are making a great gamble for great gains. It isn't right to judge such people by the "justice" of their cause. Some of you spergs and almost all of the half-educated class think when Nietzsche talks about "beyond good and evil" that he's making some grand proposition about there being no possibility to evaluate men or events. Morality is absolute necessity for the people. There is the other morality, that reveals a biological hierarchy. Just the same, a different standard applies to huemans, and a different one to the true men who are willing to live in danger, and who don't care for their animal lives. Men like Denard and Hoare are a great *attempt* on the part of nature itself: they show that even in our age there are men who yearn inscribe their wills in bronze for the ages, who want their terrible creations to endure for centuries. They should be judged by what they were willing to risk in their spirit—and also by the unequaled rush they all must have had, inside them, as they pursued their high aims. Even just a few years ago Margaret Thatcher's son Mark was given a sentence in South Africa in 2005 for an attempted coup in Equatorial Guinea. He was ratted out and caught at the airport. You must understand that the meddlesome little cretinoids who run the West always put a stop to great plans and great actions. They've ended many promising adventures through their snooping...they're tattletales, always watching, never sleeping, always whispering. Gallant men, who live under the sign of the lion are stopped before they can act. A different way is necessary. But I mean to say, don't be fooled: in our age too men of adamantine character exist, who fight like Capaneus before Thebes, ready nude with fire in arm to burn down city. They appear now as villain, now as hero to the people, but you must learn to forget just *this desire of the people* and yearn rather to live dangerously and do great deeds, for good or evil. The danger of our time is not that it makes people bad, but that it makes everything small and afraid. Neall Ellis in his trusty Mi-24 Hind helicopter held off the rebels in the Sierra Leone civil war, singlehandedly, and saved innumerable lives. There's little glamor in his job, and in the end it didn't matter: but on his trusty flying Hind steed he must have felt like a beast of prey swooping down on the enemy. He worked for company, Executive Outcomes—a name that might make you think of second-rate consulting company in office park. But this was merc company that ended the civil war in Sierra Leone and threatened to establish a new order all over Africa. For this reason they were stopped by the UN, by gangs of international lawyers and financiers who fear the power of the new Sea Peoples. How long can they hold off such men from their destiny? In the Rhodesian war, you had companies of a few white farmers, raised in the bush, who ambushed armies of Zambia and Mozambique many thousands strong. They would attack with stealth, stalking them, inflict frightful casualties, and escape unharmed. Many such stories: look up Nyadzonya raid. The potential for adventures and conquests like European man has rarely experienced in the past still exists, and I have no doubt that in the coming years such opportunities will become ever more frequent. The great Leviathan will falter, sooner or later. The coming age of barbarism will not be owned, as so many of you urban cucks fear, by the gangbangers and the unwashed hordes of the teeming cesspools of the world, but by clean-cut middle-class and working-class vets, men of military experience, who know something about how to shoot and how to organize. The fools who think oligarchs will be able to control these men for very long should look to the fortunes of the Sforzas and many others, and remember that money is no match for force of arms combined with charm.

When Theodore Roosevelt was I think close to seventy years old, he went on expedition to the Amazon, then mostly still unexplored: he called it one last chance to be a boy. This expedition led to his death; and it was a good death. He followed in footsteps of men of power like Lope de Aguirre...and never lost the yearning in his heart for Eldorado.

Part Four: a Few Arrows

63

Giving "freedom" to women—*an impossibility.* With the liberation of women in the 19th century, the West has given itself an infection from which it can't recover without the most terrible convulsions and the most thorough purgative measures. What the "freedom" of women means in practice is the domination of mankind by the demagogues who can rally the lower orders of the spirit. Because there is no world in which "the women" can act as a political unit. Liberation of women means freedom and power for financiers, lawyers, purveyors of comforts in and outside government, employers who whore out your wife and daughters. It has been the greatest weakening and self-own a civilization has ever visited on itself. But in the end is this so different from democracy as such? Yes...because the "liberation" of women makes democracy into a terminal disease...one that doesn't just end a particular government, but the civilization.

64

If you wonder how mankind fell from the high times of the Renaissance and the age of exploration to our times of mediocrity and repression...I can only tell you this, that our age is the norm in history. It takes great efforts and much good *luck* to be able to surpass the dirty ape and rat inside us all. Most of mankind never left the regime of deformity, and it's no surprise that this morass is returning. It's just a reversion to the norm. That said, there does seem to be something especially menacing about developments in our age: the ubiquity of this Leviathan, the inability to escape it. Everywhere you might become a hermit, you are reminded of it, it intrudes everywhere. And so the very success of the great men of four hundred years ago, their foundation of a new world, the great expansion of human knowledge and know-how...this ended up setting the stage for our trash-world. They succeeded beyond what they could expect, and that success is what allowed the profusion of the lower types of mankind. In nature the vital part of mankind would rule and in the beginnings of many societies it does: military brotherhoods of men rule, and physical force as well as force of personality, charisma, draw the rest in an orbit around those who possess these in the highest degree. This is all by a natural and secret pull, by instinct. There is a magic to charisma that does this, and the military-monarchical organization, the rule of the warlord, comes from desire for this in the nature of all, not from reflection and abstraction. Unfortunately some things conspire to end this original condition of mankind, which is itself no paradise and is full of strife, suffering and problems. These things are, first of all, the very success of these men in securing the conditions of life and comfort for the rest of the community. Second, the ascent, within this peacetime, of the priest, the shaman, the schemer, and the matriarch, which slowly usurp power away from the brotherhoods of young men and their captains. Spinoza explains the corruption of the Jewish people in just this way: the Hebrew "Republic" was in fact a military regime of the type I say here, a rule of the captains. But the priests took this power away and corrupted the nation to weakness. In same way something happened to the Aryans in India and in many other places. This state of things doesn't *need* to be so: the men of religion and those of power have many interests in common, and can rule together. But it often happens that the men of power become decadent and let the state drift into the hands of those who *can't* rule—and who start to resent them for this abdication. Women become also very aggressive, once real and relaxed manhood atrophies. If you imagine that women in the Muslim world, for example, are sweet and feminine...they are hungry viragos of iron will. The feminist Muslima will be a figure of much importance among them. The men in Arabia will turn gay. The Vietnamese or Chinese grandmother has her knee on the neck of the son-in-law. Thus everywhere we see that the very comforts and safety produced by the best men leads to the usurpation of society by those parts of the human spirit that are oriented instead toward a different kind of life, that everywhere that mode of the yeast wins out...and usually wins out very quickly. And in the West, whose special fate has been confused for History or Progress of the entire species, this development has taken place through the promotion of logos or reason and all the manifestations of this: the adulation of empty words, of legalism as a guide for social and political life, of the cult of science that is very far from real science. All of this has been a cover for the ascent of the blob human, of the lower orders of the spirit and is instead delivering not just the West, but all of mankind, to a condition of domestic brokenness and servility. Very concretely you see in feminism the return of pre-Aryan matriarchy. The great "Earth Mother," originally some kind of half-huemean half-cockroach creature resplendent with horrid eggs like big Amazon centipede....this seeks to re-absorb you. Of all the things that you blame for the decrepit times we live in, feminism and the "liberation" of women is both

165

the proximate and the ultimate cause. Nothing so ridiculous as the liberation of women has ever been attempted in the history of mankind. It is an act of complete insanity, disguised as "logic," "reason," presented in the most absurd legalisms about supposed "rights." The modern socialisms, the expansion of the power of the state that squashes all initiative and all life, the hypocrisy of all political life in our time—all of this is to be attributed to the participation of women in political life. I don't complain about the "freedom" or "degeneracy" that supposedly comes from this arrangement. That's all misdirection and self-flattery. The state we live in is as repressive as any oriental tyranny. But its hypocrisy is that it hides its force under the delusion of egalitarian ideals and legalistic procedures inconsistently applied. It is not women actually being free, but their "legal freedom," a practical fiction, being used by a hidden power to oppress, to dispossess, to intimidate and extort. It took one hundred years of women in public life for them to almost totally destroy a civilization.

But you would be a sperg to think that this problem can be solved by taking away women's voting power, "forcing" them into the home, or some such thing. The presence of women in public life is a spear with two tips, and can be turned on the enemy with some ease. Women, after all, can still, even in the most debased condition, be made to call on their deep passions by a great leader. They voted for Hitler, Mussolini, and many others, with some enthusiasm. The enemy who "freed" them has made use of a great weapon: he has increased his power immensely and introduced a war into the house and life of every man. But this enemy also made a gamble and I believe, ultimately, a mistake...because women more than others will set their bodies on fire with passion for a savior and be willing to abandon the fear and love of comfort on which the modern state depends...them more than others, out of a wild and stupid enthusiasm.

65

How was it possible for women to become "free" at some point in the 19th century...how did this agitation come about? From where comes the gynocracy that rules, not just as in tribal societies covertly, but that now pretends also to be in the public sphere and to demand "rights"? Who was there in the first place to give rights...and of what use is a right if it's not also a privilege? The answer to all this is a little bit more unpleasant. It's only because women lost all respect for the males of the time that there could be any *pretext* like feminism or "women's suffrage" in the first place. The loss of *respect* in general marks the modern age since 1800 or so: the loss of respect in authority, for example, that came when industrialists and bankers replaced the warrior nobility. As "decadent" as the latter had become, this class had never really lost its grace of manner, its beauty and magnificence and glamor: this made the common man more eager to submit, or to accept such leadership. But who could accept the rule of the dour economic creature that took the lead in the states at the end of the 18th century? This is why Napoleon was such an enigma for so many: he represented a man out of time, something completely unexpected in the age of middle class mediocrity and hypocritical "democracy" that was just then coming about. For this reason all the higher spirits of the 19th century, all the great artists, the writers, they threw themselves at the feet of his memory: he seemed to represent the possibility of higher aspirations in our time. You can read Stendhal for this spirit. Napoleon was an escape from the domination of the bugman that was just then beginning to take hold of the nations. Now, don't imagine I will attack "the bourgeois" ...we've declined so far even from the level of the bourgeois of that age...in our time the desolation is almost complete. This is why it's so ridiculous to hear these "conservatives" yap on about honor, or glory, or sacrifice, or any of this garbage. The respect in all institutions and all leadership classes and all traditional authority has already been lost long ago, and for good reason. It's impossible for the erased males to command any respect from the people...and still less from their women. Feminism then is the revolt of women against the outrage of democracy. They have been in a revolt against the inability of the bugman to command authority or respect. And you must understand that there is no bottom to this "freedom" or revolution. There won't be any opportunity to say "I told you so": they will *never* "learn a lesson" from their foolishness. And they resent the insecurity you have put them in. The calamity that will surely follow from going down this path will not be a "teachable moment" to anyone. They resent the "beta," but you're wrong to think it was ever any different. No...great civilizations and cultures were never founded nor kept alive by "betas." The nerdoids who have taken over much of the right have brainwashed you to this view, but it's wrong. Women never loved the shopkeeper, the timid merchant with the nasal voice, and no, not even the clockmaker or craftsman. They have always loved the knight, the sailor in love with wild ideas of the sea, the adventurer and pirate. And it is right that they loved these men, and that, with the coming of the rule of the bugman, they would try to seek their "liberation" from unworthy men and the boring society they were building. That this resentment was manipulated itself by the Satanic power that rules our time, and that through this very drive for freedom woman became enslaved more than she had been before…is beside the point. You won't be able to make women "see reason" and love a "beta civilization"—a fabrication of the HBD cuckold crowd of our time. Women will love you if you are a warrior. And they will help, through the entirely retarded mechanism of democracy, to elect men of glamor and charisma who are our only immediate hope against the machine that runs our garbage world. Trump, for all his hesitations, is only the beginning. He has shown the path insofar as woman is concerned. The mob also is a woman. Now imagine a man of Trump's charisma, but who is not merely beholden to the generals, but one of them, and able to rule and intimidate them as well as seduce the many. So far we have only had Gracchi …but Caesars and Napoleons are sure to follow.

66

A man of great charisma who can seduce the people with a wild spirit and *break through* the rule of the pervasive bureaucracy-media complex is our best hope for the immediate problem…and maybe our only hope. Such a man might be among you and, in any case, he will need help. Our enemy has so much spread: he is everywhere. He's in your home even, and he's inside you. The domain of the fight has extended everywhere now. Therefore any answer must be on multiple fronts, and each one calls for a different strategy and different type of talent and man. I fear that many of you are actually autists and spergs and don't want to see this. There is no one fight and no one solution, and what you want in the end or as ideal may require different plan than facing imminent threat. For the latter you can make alliance with people who otherwise wouldn't be your friends. I believe that democracy is the final cause of all the political problems I describe here, but in the short run democracy—the will of the people—is on our side because the democracies have been hijacked by a stupid and corrupt elite. The nations face extinction and an era of permanent civil war because this elite wants to pillage and pillage: and wants to flood them with the shit of the world. This is the immediate threat, and on this you can be allied with people who otherwise may not shoot for the same star you do. If Ann Coulter or Pat Buchanan were in charge, you would get 99% of what you want. Therefore use them as models to solve the problems that face you, and don't scare the peoples with crazy talk if you want to move things politically. Let the normies have their normal lives, and paint our enemies as the crazies...which they are...and as the corrupt vermin they are. If you haven't compromised yourself go into political life maybe, and use Trump as a model for success. Those of you who choose this path, if you like this book or the other things I say, should denounce it and disavow me if ever asked about it, and denounce also all other crazy ideas. You must have an instinct for how much normies are able to take. It isn't even a question of getting them to where you want "gradually"—I don't think they're able to get very far at all. But they can be moved to defend themselves from the grip of the global slave state, which I also hate, although for different reasons. If an ethnostate is your ideal, or if it's Renaissance Switzerland or ancient Egypt—fine. If you intend to go public and try something politically, work now instead so that America and Europe don't become Bosnia or South Africa. People who try to mislead you from such things and try to encourage you to talk *in public* instead about abstractions like "ethnostate," dork ideological constructs like "Eurasianism," anachronistic slogans like "blood and soil" that never had any historical attraction to Anglos and Americans...these people are spergs or very often federal informants, or manipulated by such. By all means study such things, believe in them, troll with them, let them guide your final aims; but know what is possible in the normie political sphere and don't become the clown of ZOG like Nehlen and so many others did. If they were serious people they would have never come in public and encouraged young men to go on marches where they could be identified and tracked for life. Know when the snake is defending itself—don't be a patsy. Your models must be those *that have worked:* Trump, Orban, the Italian movements now ascendant, Sebastian Kurz and his party in Austria. You don't see these people marching around in hotel bellboy's uniforms with a *Sonnenrad* and talking about the "Jewish Question" and this other kind of role-play. It's true that in the end, my aims here and those of someone like Orban have little or nothing in common. If they were successful, all they would be able to do is reestablish the same world of sheep that existed a hundred years ago, maybe inoculated against the latest degradations...but nothing very great. Still, I think it's better for the nations to be well-tended, happy sheep than to be reduced to teeming piles of starving rats. This, anyway, is my advice for those who want to go into normie politics and have a relatively normie life, and there's nothing wrong with that—it's even a great necessity.

I've written this book, however, because this may not satisfy some of us, and I wanted to talk about the world in the coming decades, and what paths may open for a different way.

67

Too much is already said about the evils of suburbs, but I think the danger of such places for modern civilized man is so great that it must be repeated. On the other hand it's important not to take this too far: the Europeans live in the center of their cities and are politically and socially in just as bad or worse situations. Still, I think it's easier for them to fix their problems, and to avert the greatest dangers, should they arrive. It's easier because in these places the rightful citizens of the nations still own their cities. I don't see any evidence that the tax base of America moved to the suburbs by choice. Their inner cities were taken away from them not, as is imagined, by blacks, but by the politicians—and their handlers—who found it more profitable to replace middle class citizens with an underclass. The space to which they've been segregated and to which they have to "commute" is I think a form of absolute hell to raise children in, especially boys. There is no freedom of motion except to regimented activities, they are always watched by caretakers of some kind. The places are of incredible ugliness, which takes away also from the will to discover new things at all. There are no nooks and corners where boys can form gangs, be away from prying eyes of parents and others, and have the feeling that they are exploring and owning territory, as there is in the city and in the countryside. America has successfully portioned off its historical population, its rightful citizens, and its tax base, in work camps and dormitories. That is what the modern American "city" is: an economic zone arranged much like a work-camp, or concentration-camp if you want. It would be trivial for the French security services to shut off access to the *banlieues* infested by turds, and it would be just as trivial for American security services to shut off access to the suburbs and hold the middle class by the neck. I think the reason the suburbs are hateful to the raising of boys is also the reason they are most objectionable in general, namely that while in the countryside or the city a restive population would be able to hold their territory and challenge a power should the need arise, such a thing is impossible in the suburbs. Suburbs are living arrangement for slaves and subjects.

68

"Social justice"—disgusting parasitism, dressed up in rags of words so worn-out and pee-stained even their defenders are sick of the smell...they say it half-mouthed and pleading: just look at them during the Occupy rallies, hoping to siphon off *respect.* The *need* to be *respected* is sign of very low and wormlike condition of spirit. The tantrums of the coddled and domesticated, of no force... No force behind it, just the opinions of the left-over, the prattling of guilt and begging: not even the Marxist engine of the worker. What worker? They have contempt for the worker...the force and confidence in his labor, in the place of his labor in history that the Bolshevik had is gone, now it's the lumpen using his language, unconvincingly. Dependent on the Leviathan, and therefore its tool. "Social" justice...but why only "social"...why set your sights so low...you mean just the opinions of the many? Who cares. Here is *my* vision of the true justice, the justice of nature: the zoos opened, predators unleashed by the dozens, hundreds....four thousand hungry wolves rampaging on streets of these hive cities, elephants and bison stampeding, the buildings smashed to pieces, the cries of the human bug shearing through the streets as the lord of beasts returns. Manhattan, Moscow, Peking reduced to ruins overgrown by vines and forest, the haunt of the lynx and coyote again. The great cesspool slums, Calcutta, Nairobi, all the fetid latrines of the world covered over by mudslides, overgrown with thick jungle, this is justice. Lisbon to me always seemed city still inhabited just out of *vanity*. Let loose hundreds of tigers, companies of rhinoceros, with strong engine of spirit revving in their deep chests, let them bring the justice of the volcano to this world of trash! Bless the passing of the Shoggoth!

69

There is story from Heian period in Japanese history that I always found amazing. Japan was still ruled by the Imperial court and there were local administrators and so on, like any Oriental centralized despotism. But there was also warrior class. They inherited this from some steppe invasions that changed their society a few centuries before. Anyway as always happens, the Imperial bureaucrats grew useless and weak and by the end of this age, all the actual physical power was with the samurai. What I find amazing is how long it took them to figure out they no longer had to listen to the weak commands of the Imperial hierarchy, and that they were actually the rulers. Words like "legitimacy," "soft power," "rights," or, in their time honor, duty, divine right and so on are all delusions meant to distract and obscure men of power from their own strength and aims, and put them in service to someone else. Such men are more likely than others to be driven by notions of honor and responsibility. And this sense is therefore very easy to abuse...and such men can be manipulated for some time. Eventually they do realize, however, that they don't have to listen, and that they are actually the ones who rule. This moment, when "the game is up," the moment of revelation, is what I've always found very amazing. In the modern world everything moves much faster....I expect that not long from now such men will awaken in the West and I suppose other parts of the world, and wonder why for so long they had listened to complete cretins give orders...and give orders too with such weak pretexts, much weaker than the bureaucracy of Imperial Japan. In Fiji the natives became relatively recently outnumbered because a hundred years before the English imported their favorite cheap labor, the Tamils. Eventually these outbred the natives and became the majority. So under democracy rules, they took over the state. The natives, however, still controlled the military. They saw no reason why they must follow this "democracy" into giving their lands away to aliens brought in by oppressors. So they took over the state, and did so very easily. I think it's inevitable that this will become the rule all over the world, and very soon. Democracy and ethnic diversity don't mix, but the ethnic nationalists are wrong when they think that the result of all this will be secession. Low-grade ethnic warfare is a terrible thing, but to break up entire nations into smaller pieces, as much as the city state is to my taste, isn't likely to happen. You must look to South Africa where the whites and coloreds could have asked for their own state in Cape Town, and agitated for this, but instead they wanted to keep the country together. The reason for this is that any such secession would have meant giving up all parts of the country rich in gold, diamonds, and many other things. South Africa is an extreme case and secession, where a minority is five or ten percent of the population....here it *might* happen. But it's a net loss to have the Boers migrate out of the land their ancestors tamed and built, and it would be a net loss in America if it had to happen what some of you want, to cede the southwest to Mexico, or whatever other schemes are discussed. If indeed you do manage to get a white population that is as mobilized and self-aware as you want, they won't feel it a great victory to give up land and resources their ancestors won by their valor. The greatest president was Polk. But what's likely to happen long before any mobilization by white populations in their home countries is military rule: democracy will go before pure ethnostates are formed. I think this happened many times in history in ages of national decline, not just because of ethnic or religious diversity, but for many other reasons, and most of all because the military form of government is natural to human species. Those generals will be most successful who mix power with personal flair, like Duterte or Peron did. This is very difficult in America because of the types of men who get promoted in the military. Some will be able to affect, however, the charisma of Roman stern old man.

70

Given the inevitability of military government, I see already how nationalists and many similar men, sympathetic to the cause of freedom and high life, will join the armed forces and rise through the ranks, and my guess is that many are already doing this. In some way this had already happened, and at the middle ranks the armed forces are still relatively full of patriots throughout the western world. In France the military and security services, including the CRS, support the National Front of Le Pen, overwhelmingly. It's only a matter of time. In the Anglo world it's somewhat more complicated. The upper ranks have long been purged of men who could offer resistance to the hidden hands that rule: it started with the Tailhook "scandal," and even before then, and only accelerated after. Even at the level of captain or major, many men are traditional conservatives and not exactly nationalists. I think it's unnecessary to address such men directly: events alone will convince them. But many are being persecuted as it is, and run out of the military, in the same way that police departments are being purged. This process is very slow. It won't work out well in the end for the lords of lies: all the technology in the world won't save a "diverse" military if it should ever be in a conflict: they'll turn the missiles on themselves by accident or run submarines into the ocean floor, as has already happened in South Africa. Still, America is pretty well isolated from danger, and you fool yourself if you think they will "reform" anything even if they suffer disastrous defeats abroad. They fear men of power within the country more than they do any foreign army. It's difficult to solve this problem. The military is already so full of homofaggotry that it will be very unpleasant for any man who is a man to join its ranks at the moment. He might have a hard time advancing in its hierarchy, even affecting the views of a traditional religious conservative or a mainstream Trumpist which is, I suppose, as far as you could go right now. I would hate also to see any free man killed or maimed in the service of this military that's been turned into a Hessian merc force for Gulf nabobs, for various ethnic groups, for the idiotic schemes of international financiers and the benefit of machine politicians looking to advance their families' fortunes abroad. Then there is also the extreme *boredom* you should expect from any kind of military life, which even under the best circumstances consists in busywork. That said, military training is very valuable. Even in a situation—precisely in the case where men of any worth will have a tough time becoming generals and such...then it will be even more valuable. Military training and the brotherhood with other men in battle that comes from it is a lifelong advantage, and a great benefit to any cause. I can't give advice to anyone for how to live, but those who would be willing to deal with the evils of the modern military and are aware of all the drawbacks, but still find themselves suited for it, would do a great good for themselves and for their peoples if they joined. It goes without saying that they will have to practice good judgment and discretion while in service; but the military can't simply be abandoned to mohawked Latinx traps and neo-Leninist activists. Nationalists, I have no doubt, will join and attempt to reform both the ranks and the academies in the western world. Then there are also things like the French Foreign legion, although the discipline they practice is terrible. It lasts seven years, and they reserve the right to pursue you in any country if you desert. Many ex-SS men and other Germans from World War II joined the legion and fought in Vietnam, and some committed suicide because of the rigors of this unit. Although it's possible now that they've relaxed somewhat.

71

Everything that is said now about Russia is pure projection. In fact it's America and the western world that is run by spooks and intel agencies. They've placed their assets and compromised patsies in the corporate world no less than in other government agencies and among elected politicians. Many, like Obama for example, are entirely creations of this or that faction inside the security system. These in turn are allied to oligarchs and often to foreign interests and powers, so that it's hard to think many western nations have anything but a parody of freedom and national sovereignty. "Representative democracy" plus a bureaucratic state is often criticized by conservatives as destructive of personal freedom and initiative, which it is; but given that most people who go into public life are poor and weak-minded, it also just means indirect rule by spooks, oligarchs, and whatever foreign nation or interest can funnel more money or influence or threat here or there. Many of these people in the west screaming about Russia are puppets of China or the Gulf States—even when they're not directly on the take or compromised, they expect sinecures and great wealth that will come in the future. Most of the media is similarly compromised, although the average schmuck journalist is probably deluded by the platitudes of "free press" and the humanitarian doxies that have been banged in their heads. Inside head they have central vacuole full of fluid, no brain. I have no doubt that things *like* "pizzagate" are real simply because, if I was a spook, or a rich man with spooks available, I'd find it very easy to compromise the officious, status-hungry *low* people who have been attracted to government in our time. These people arrive in the capital cities with a hungry look in the eye and, being full of the feeling that "they're in on things" and that they've made it, have a very tough time controlling their appetites or behavior. Many are chosen and groomed precisely because they begin with demented appetites to begin with. This isn't to say there aren't patriotic factions within the security services that actually run the west, or patriotic oligarchs who can't offshore their wealth, and whose interest is in some sense then tied to the land and the people. I foresee a time anyway when nationalists, those who are capable of it, will begin to join these services. They will do themselves, their friends, and their country a great good through this. Some who are suited to math and technology will no doubt join those types of agencies. Others are already learning foreign languages— Tibetan has many uses! But there are other languages and area studies for those who go to college, to study and do well in. Arabic, Russian, Persian, Chinese,

Indonesian—many opportunities! Given the very low talent pool in government or available for recruitment, they will be able to join *those other* types of agencies, of which there are a few, with some ease. Here it would be necessary more than in the military to hide one's power level, and even to affect the left-internationalist doxy at times. Any nationalist or populist would be wise to affect at most the style of a Mueller should he want to be "on the right." Not all are capable of this, and I think the strain will be considerable. Such people will often have to work alone and remain quite isolated for years, holding their aim and star as a precious hidden possession, and never confuse the short-term for the final goal. Few will be able to or want to deal with the nonsense...this has been the problem of the Anglo conservatives all along, though. They've always preferred to get a tan, play tennis, and make money. They've wanted to be left alone, so that the state was taken over by vermin. I expect such things will change, regardless of what I or anyone else says, simply because some people want to survive, and not to die out. They will no doubt slowly, one way or another, join and change the face of such agencies. The power of the modern world remains, for the foreseeable future, in such agencies. A fateful comet like a Caesar and Napoleon is a hard thing to hope for. And such a man would need allies, anyway.

72

Government work can be too boring for men of adventure. Some say that the CIA, for example, exaggerates its incompetence in movies, or in known events—the failure of 9/11, of Iraq, their endless humiliations at the hands of the Soviets—to hide its true power and appear weaker than it is. But I think this isn't true, and if you've met ex-CIA people you'll understand that the rumors about their disability aren't exaggerated at all. After James Jesus Angleton they were thoroughly fucked in every hole by the Soviets and others. All his warnings came true. He was a unique American, of rare secretive character in a people that enjoys openness and display; for this he is now maligned in mean-spirited movies. He wasn't very typical of his people, the Anglo-Saxon, and I suppose it's possible that through his Spanish blood there came a strain of Habsburg court intrigue, or something like this. The Russians and others are very good at intelligence work, because they grow up in a world of secrecy and learn to take *great joy* in subterfuge of this kind. Most Americans who try this are just playing games, and affecting a manner. Full of Mormons and various cripplettes who put on a *high Wasp manner,* full also of soccer moms and neuters, the intelligence services are in fact quite incompetent, despite their considerable power. Both can be true. And you can see this in their very clumsy attempts to affect public opinion inside America. I won't talk about speculation over false flag attacks and such, which I'm sure happen. But it's without a doubt that they've tried to get into the "meme" business, and had units dedicated to this kind of visual propaganda, especially during the last election. We all saw their efforts and we laughed. I think the biggest threat the right presented to this system came from something like 4chan, which showed it can be an intelligence agency of its own, and far superior to what the formal spooks could do. How they located obscure objects, places, and people from photos is something that formally-trained agents couldn't normally do. The *memes* put a spike of fear in the hearts of all the constipated spooks. A couple of images spread by Ricky Vaughn or some channers made the news and were many times more effective than the government's own propaganda efforts, and you can see, in shows like *Homeland* and others, the really titanic hatred these people had for the army of right-wing autists that messed up their plans. They work hard to dox, for this reason. You must understand where your strengths lie. If government or military work isn't appropriate, learn this art of the visual communication and share it with your friends, work with each other to perfect it. Don't be lame. Learn to make videos and photos—there are various tools around, many editing programs. You can start with cheap camera if you need. Work in groups...in "labs" to develop, perfect, and target these videos and images. I assure you this frightens them, and is many, many times more effective than marching in public and playing the clown they want you to play. The long game of persuading the public is far from won. Keep the eye on the task, far from accomplished: to discredit authorities, to mock all public pieties, to show the leaders of government, bureaucracy, finance, corporations, big tech, and media for the pathetic ghouls they are. Many gains have been made lately, but their dishonor in the eyes of the normies is far from accomplished. When they try to make you expose yourself and to make positive claims, they win. Keep up the pressure of true *samizdat.*

73

Some people like to meet and display in public, and I think this can be done, if done well. But there are very few groups that do this well. They exist all over the world—a couple in America and Europe, some in South America and in Japan. The few nationalist organizations that do it well have much care for appearance and also don't engage in ideologies, symbols and behaviors that are bizarre or hostile to the customs and wishes of the people. A Japanese nationalist can invoke Shinto imagery and oppose this nationalist mode to the "foreign" religion of Buddhism, but that's because these two traditions have been in a push-pull game throughout the history of that country, and still are. But no independent pagan tradition exists in the western world, and play-acting in that way is going to fail. Offending Christians in political movements is stupid, when they're one of the last bastions against a common enemy. If their beliefs are corrupted, they can be reformed. Above all I believe that any public movement will be most effective if it is *not* political at all, and remains "implicit." I think there can be much good done in public, but should be promoted in the form of a social movement, not a political one. Nationalists must present a healthy alternative to the eternal rule of ugliness in our time: promote nature, beauty, physical fitness, the preservation of high traditions of literature and art. In regards to the latter, it's even a necessity because there's no school or university that will give you a worthwhile education. There are a variety of ways to approach this but I think given the collapse of the Boy Scouts, that a scouting and nature-preservation movement would be one of the best. Hiking and the protection, preservation, and admiration of public and national parks would put youth in the wilderness and inspire a sense of boundlessness and awe in them. It would teach them many skills, build camaraderie, and emphasize the connection between the people and the land both for the participants and as a matter of image for others. It's without a doubt that *any* public organization will be infiltrated by feds, hostiles, and *agents provocateurs,* and therefore it's necessary to avoid and condemn any imagery or message of violence, and to ostracize people who exhibit tendencies in that direction or who try to convince others to idiotic "action." One can do this at the same time that such groups can engage in self-defense martial arts training and indeed, in an urban setting, work for the creation of private boxing and wrestling clubs. The risks are considerable either way, but it's not out of the question that through the path of the promotion of health and beauty you will be able even to persuade feds to your side: they too can self-improve! This would be a movement of peace. The right can at the moment furthermore easily take over the doctrine of peace—of nonintervention abroad—and of the protection of nature, and these things would be great achievements...this would go some way to convincing youth to your side. I would also recommend that you don't engage in outright racism of a useless sort, for example, the deliberate exclusion of friendlies from different races and so on; they would in any case be very few. This can happen at the same time that you openly appeal to white youths and defend them from racial attacks and teach them the greatness of their history and their literary traditions. Women, on the other hand, must be absolutely excluded from such groups, and rather encouraged to have their own. The presence of women in any group like this will totally destroy its social function, by introducing sexual competition, and by the fact that it's in their blood to play on men's misplaced chivalry to cause friction for their own advantage. Such a movement would be a living rebuke to the constrained and *low*, anxious life promoted by the regime of the crippled. Once developed and with some reach, but maybe even in the beginning, they can engage in local welfare projects of various kinds, for example helping opiate addicts by providing them with gyms and by breathing into them the desire for life, helping old people who are alone, keeping the streets and parks clean, and many other such things. I also think that claiming public spaces in cities should eventually be tried, in the same way that members of Generation Identity in Europe often patrol the subways and streets to show they won't be intimidated. But for this to happen there must be good-will built first for the public. There will of course be many attacks made on such groups, but what matters is whether the majority will *believe* them. If you remain firm as a social movement of peace, of the promotion of natural beauty, healthy living, and healthy nationalism, any attacks on such groups can be made to appear for what they are, the fears of the paranoids and hatreds of the resentful and ugly.

74

The equivalent of the "meme" in political action is the *prank*. You really can't underestimate the power of a good prank...this can be as little as putting up a funny banner or a witty slogan. Such things don't need to be connected to any formal group, but done in private by yourself or with your friends. The pit bull ban campaign is a great example of real-life trolling. The "It's OK to be white" stickers were a good idea, at least in the beginning: those who began to put threatening fonts on them, or logos for weirdo organizations ruined that troll very fast. The purpose of all such "political action" should be the same as memetic *samizdat*, which is to make the enemy look ridiculous. You must show them for what they are, which is, dour, old, sclerotic, ugly, pedantic; it's good if you show yourself in the opposite light, although not necessary. But in France the Hommen, a traditionalist and manly response to the Femmen, have provided a good model for attractive public action of this sort. They use masks, and anonymity is often an absolute necessity for this kind of thing. But the possibilities of this are boundless and, even in cases like the "OK to be white" stickers, where the initial message isn't funny, it works because it forces the enemy to take a public position that is widely and justly recognized as evil and resentful. Trump has been very good at this, although it's not hard; he frequently forces his opponents to take the side of the vilest murderers, gang members, of lawlessness and decrepit viciousness. All such actions must be performed unannounced, planned in secret, and carried out with a close group of friends, to prevent the enemy from organizing a preemptive action. Remember that they still own many of the cities and the police forces in these cities, which can be induced to act illegally and to put you in danger; for this reason, and many others, public rallies announced well ahead of time are totally useless, as are public "policy" speeches and other such wankery. You must of course avoid all violence and all talk of violence as well, and not fall into the trap they want you to fall into. In a small group of friends you know yourself, it's easier to police who stays and who doesn't, and easier to use your judgment about whether this or that guy is nuts or worse. Remember always to keep eyes on the prize in such action, which is to discredit the enemy and expose his authoritarianism, his stupidity, his slavishness, his corruption.

75

The friends you make are more important, far more important, than the girlfriends or wives you'll have. And actually your girl will admire you for this—not that you should do it for that reason, but it's an added benefit: women admire men with great personal projects, and who are not beholden to them. If she's your "everything" and your "best friend," she will likely lose respect for you. The greatest "in" that nationalists and allies have against the enemy is the fact that the enemy has sowed sexual chaos and has destroyed romance. Our parents' generations are largely responsible for this, but the lords of lies and ugliness who rule our time continue it and use it as their greatest tool of control. So this is the best way to awaken men to the evil and subjection of our time, and, I would say, also many women, who are very unsatisfied. On the other hand, someone who is motivated simply by this problem isn't reliable. There won't be any "beta revolution," and betas are unreliable, because they can be easily bought off with a girlfriend, or even a shrew wife and the parody of a good domestic life. I've seen many men, intelligent and well-educated, but weak in their core and much too concerned with women, who gave up all higher aspirations once a half-decent girl came along. I find it disturbing that so many think this kind of life is a great salvation for you personally or "for your race." This is ridiculous. By all means, marry and have children if you want, but don't do it as a political statement or a form of action. Quite aside from the fact that you yourself wouldn't have wanted to be born as part of a demographic war, this isn't a kind of struggle that civilized races, with a need for space and fresh air, can ever win. The idea that whites or Japanese should start vomiting out six or seven children to a vagina like the illiterate slave hordes of Bangladesh or Niger is absurd. For one, it's never going to happen...and it shouldn't. Throughout history we've almost always been outnumbered, and it hasn't been a problem. Immigration restriction, combined with some judicious deportation done gradually, would be enough to secure the homelands of the civilized. If the situation worsens or a time of crisis comes, the eventual abandonment of democracy and other, far sterner measures, including, I expect, the intervention of the military, will take place. Autists having a family or not doesn't matter in a world of billions; the European nations have populations of hundreds of millions and aren't in danger of "dying out." So by all means, have a girlfriend and a family, but I fear that too much focus on this as a "statement" against the program of the enemy is a mistake. Usually a family is the end of a man. This can be both good and bad. But the necessities of caring for a family, and the emotional demands, usually blind him to anything higher. In case you do have a family, have it because you have great love and lust for a woman—and I would recommend the same for women, abandonment to such instinct, if you are lucky enough to have it. Choose by quality of biology and remember that the intellect is inherited from the mother, the character from the father. But once you have a family, don't think this is a "political" achievement, or that it would ever be enough. Continue the mission you have set out for yourself, and continue above all the friendships you have formed in service to this higher cause. The friendships you have made meeting each other, in person or online, are the greatest event of the last few years, and source for the greatest promise. You must never stop studying and working together or forget the enthusiasm of this discovery. A friendship in struggle for war and a higher cause is something that, more than anything else, can lift you out of the dreadful gravity of this turgid world of shades.

76

Caring too much about food, nutrition, and especially health can be considered something unmanly...a kind of neurotic, hypochondriac fretting more suited to spinsters. On the other hand, in the past the world was not as full of poison as it is now. Nearly all the food is centrally produced, stored in warehouses, and poisoned with mycotoxins and many other things that slowly destroy your essence. Therefore it's important to take measures to protect yourself against this as far as you can. Although it's expensive, the probiotic Gastrus has been of great use to many of us. Something else I can recommend is coconut oil, and staying in the sun. If you are not a bogjig whose ancestors evolved under permanent cloud cover in northwest Europe, you will usually be able to tan, and the effects of sun are many and very good. You have no excuse! (Those who can't tan must supplement with vitamin D3, but also some other things.) You begin with ten minutes in mid-day sun, and work up from there. Usually thirty minutes a day is enough, when you can get there. There's much propaganda about tanning, but once you live in tropical areas you can see that even brown people begin to look sickly and have a kind of sallow color if they avoid the sun. You're meant to worship the sun. Remember the song of New Order! It goes without saying that you must lift weights, and for this there are many different programs, all suited to a different body, different biology, and different aims. In general it's better to lose fat and cut body fat before growing in muscle, but it depends on many things. But a regime of sun and steel is absolutely required, for your mood, your aesthetics, for getting the attention of women and the respect of men, and above all for preparation for struggle and war. In ancient Greek cities, only the citizens were allowed to lift weights and work in the gym: slaves were forbidden. It's no wonder that the robots of Babylon seek to ban gyms for men in our time. The pathetic failure of the "swole-left," an entirely artificial construct promoted in a pre-planned and coordinated way by formal organs of the left, all of this is very instructive: the occasional exception aside, it's not possible to be "swole-left" today. Any man who improves his body through sun and steel will drift away from the modern left, a program of decrepitude and resentful monstrosity. They know this and are afraid.

I have to make this restatement now at the end of this brief manifesto:

Many are domestic animals and happy that way. I speak instead to the men who feel stifled by this bug world.

People at all times try to domesticate each other. Language is used to clobber and deceive others into submission and domestication. Ideas and arguments and stories are manufactured for the same. The modern world is no different in this regard from any wretched tribal society. I'm sure that Europe prior to the Bronze Age, before the coming of the Aryans, was similar to modern Europe. People lived in communal longhouses and were likely browbeaten and ruled by obese mammies who instilled in them socialism and feminism.

Most of those so-called males of the longhouse age were probably similar to the modern leftist "herb" who doesn't lift. Which is why those societies were so easily conquered.

The left realizes they look weak and lame—because they are. They know they have nothing to offer youth but submission and lectures. They know they're unsexy and staid. If indeed young leftist men will start lifting and worshiping beauty, they will be forced to leave the left.

The bugman pretends to be motivated by compassion, but is instead motivated by a titanic hatred of the well-turned-out and beautiful. The bugman seeks to bury beauty under a morass of ubiquitous ugliness and garbage. So much of the Pacific and the pristine oceans are now full of garbage and plastic. This garbage is flowing out of cities built on piles of unimaginable filth. The waters are polluted with birth control pills and mind-bending drugs emitted by obese high-fructose-corn-syrup-guzzling beasts. Then of course there is the ugliness of the people. And it's only getting uglier with the crowded, unhygienic new cities of our age, populated by hordes of dwarf-like zombies that are imported for slave labor and political agitation from the fly-swept latrines of the world.

People feel they can't escape this, they know this is an aggressive method to demoralize and oppress. When I post my images of vitality in the clear sun of a long noon, they feel a weight lifted off them. Many feel as if they've escaped the gravity of this trash world and returned to a time when the natural beauty of man could be displayed, indicating this is a form of life free to develop its powers.

I believe in the right of nature. I'm bored by ideology and by wordchopping. The images I post speak for themselves and point to a primal order that is felt by all, in a physical sense.

When I or my followers post powerful, beautiful images of male models of unbelievable vitality and youth, our enemies gnash their teeth in envy and hatred, while we are exalted and inspired.

The superior, like the handsome Alexander, exert an almost magical effect that draws others to them. Some are drawn to higher action, others to other tasks, but all petty cares are forgotten. There is nothing that needs to be said or elaborated, no need to intellectualize this any more than the natural attraction wolves on the move have for their king, or bees in a hive for their queen.

When I post images of godlike men like Pietro Boselli, many are in awe and drawn to emulate. I have inspired many to develop their bodies and physical and spiritual power.

I have nothing to say to the frivolous people who have found themselves, maybe bewildered, in positions of influence in media or government, or to the many superfluous who follow them. In the next hundred years and even before, barbaric piratical brotherhoods will wipe away this corrupt civilization, as they did at the end of the Bronze Age.

77
The Star of the Covenant—

What is likely then to happen in the long run? I foresee a time, not too far in the future, when the Leviathan will not be able to hold itself together. I expect that the peoples will be able to save themselves from the global slave project that is now promoted. But what will come after is likely to be unsatisfying as well. The nations will escape the danger, but they will return to their peaceful and sheep-like existence. They will need to be protected from getting themselves into the same position as they are now. I believe that at some point, before or after the troubles, the superior specimens are going to find each other and leave this civilization. They will form fortresses on the edge of the civilized world, in the tropics, from where they will watch the seas. The era of high piracy will return. Such men will develop above all their physical powers and their ability to wage war. They will offer the nations defense in exchange for a price. Occasionally they will send a great demagogue into the peoples, when this becomes necessary. Such men, perched atop these eagles' nests, will have the territory of a new frontier again, and a life that suits them. Science will be liberated from the constraints of caring for comfort or entertainment. Great projects in science, the projects of private men, will once again begin. Such fortresses will possess frightful weapons to defend themselves, and will have penetrated deep into the nations their antennae and their many emissaries and watchers.

I think that is a great dream, but it may happen sooner than you think. With a few details off, it's what Executive Outcomes would have become, or Bob Denard would have become, if the great states of Europe had been unable to stop them. And I think soon they will be unable. But this great opportunity is still some time away. Before then, there must be a great work done. I see a time soon when a few men, maybe no more than a few hundred in the whole nation, or spread out over the whole world, will embark on the mission of the great down-going. I have praised instinct many times in this book. But life on the ascent can follow instinct, whereas if you feel yourself to be a decadent, it's very important to resist instincts that lead to pointless self-destruction. Discipline and excellence are best when they come from your own desires, not from repression. But if your instincts lead you instead to self-debasing behaviors that will hurt you, by all means resist. Just understand that this path is at most a makeshift. We should want to give birth to beings who follow the higher path in life as a matter of innate blood and desire, not out of duty. Having to spend time and spiritual energy trying to repress destructive desires is difficult and expensive. Discipline is most important, but it matters where it comes from. Unfortunately many pay no attention at all to these two ways of "discipline," but instead are concerned only with the public image of their virtue or goodness. There's next to no good in that. And the right has hurt itself considerably by the adoption of this kind of Phariseeism. I give you an example of what I mean: many of the intelligence agencies are populated with Mormons. These men are chosen for their upright moral character, the fact that they pass lie detector tests, that they're not easily compromised, and so on...all qualities that make for *bad spies.* To be effective in this world you must be very well-acquainted with the underworld, with criminal life, with junkies, dealers, prostitutes, gamblers, with the perviest of pervs. And this is what I mean by the great down-going. To gain a true hold on the foundations of this trash-world, a certain group among the right will have to descend in this inferno. I am firmly convinced that this is the key to overturning everything that is corrupt, and the path to the great purgation. I imagine a network of brothels and gambling-houses around the world, production of porn videos, and a complete penetration of the world of vice. Yes, to ensnare, to compromise, to corrupt, and above all *to observe and to know their secrets.* To descend into a floating world of complete vice, and even to engage in it—as you must if you are to thrive in this world—while keeping your head and keeping in focus the fire of your aim...isn't this a great and very difficult achievement? This path must be only for very few, very few are suited to it. But these few are to be among the greatest of the coming generation. This brotherhood will work instead to intensify vice, to stir up demonic passions, to sow total confusion in the heart of the beast. The increase of chaos, confusion and pressure on the Leviathan will lay it low: imagine even a world where the people, under relentless assault of contradictory and wild claims, would lose all faith in the media and government and doctors and believe *nothing* they hear through official channels anymore. This would be an order of knights of the spirit such as exists at most every thousand years. Slowly, maybe over two generations, they will work patiently, exploring and laying claims to all the sewers of the underworld, all the effluences of the Leviathan, all the joints of the lower skeleton that undergirds this world. They will take over night clubs, bars, brothels, hotels, casinos, pornography, and much worse, and rather than live to insulate themselves from the vice promoted by this world, they will intensify it and learn to wield it as a great weapon. It is the greatest weapon in our age. Know that the Leviathan sustains itself not by the promotion of vice, but by its normalization. But in every normalization, a great deal must be edited out; this is its great weakness. This order of knights will *keep vice true to itself.* From underneath comes all the Satanic power of the Babylon we are fighting. Some men, whose bond between each other must be made of titanium, will surely come around who can descend in that world...who have the mental and spiritual resources to descend to the underworld and come back with the prize. I am sure this covenant, this brotherhood of the damned, when they are first taking steps to descend... will feel like the great mystery of things will reveal itself in its fullness to them...not the answer, ungraspable by the mind, but just this X, the madness inherent behind things will show itself as they are about to descend ...it will be an amazing rush, like when great pterodactyl cryptid bird of prey in Congo is about to swoop down in the night on its target from canopy. I know such men of bronze exist...I dream that, as they descend they will keep their eyes above on the great North Star, and I think about how they will feel...I imagine how they will traverse the great labyrinth of shadows while their spirit fixes itself with a great focus and obsession on that fateful star, and that other one...the destroyer of nations... never forgetting the way back....not forgetting its call and the eternal task it whispers into those with ears to listen.

Made in the USA
Middletown, DE
21 October 2023